The
Lizard

An Owner's Guide To

A HAPPY HEALTHY PET

Howell Book House

Howell Book House
A Simon & Schuster Macmillan Company
1633 Broadway
New York, NY 10019

Macmillan Publishing books may be purchased for business or sales promotional use. For information please write: Special Markets Department, Macmillan Publishing USA, 1633 Broadway, New York, NY 10019.

Cataloging-in-Publication Data available upon request from the Library of Congress

ISBN 0-87605-429-7

Manufactured in the United States of America

10 9 8 7 6 5 4 3 2 1

Series Director: Amanda Pisani
Assistant Director: Jennifer Liberts
Book Design: Michele Laseau
Cover Design: Iris Jeromnimon
Illustration: Laura Robbins and Bryan Towse
Photography:
  Front cover photo by Bill Love; back cover photo by B. Everett Webb
  Joan Balzarini: 22, 31, 33, 52, 115, 121
  Kevin Grenard: 34, 70, 83, 88, ,103
  J. Harris: 94
  Bill Love: i, 5, 9, 13, 17, 20, 26, 37, 40, 44, 45, 47, 49, 51, 57, 60, 61, 71, 76, 78, 107, 108, 114, 118, 119, 122
  L. Puente: 11, 27, 32, 38, 41, 42, 62, 73, 75, 105, 113, 117
  S. Schafer: 7
  Al Swanson: 6, 55, 86, 109
  B. Everett Webb: 2–3, 12, 25, 28–29, 30, 36, 50, 58, 65, 67, 80–81, 82, 96, 98, 100, 101
Production Team: Stephanie Hammett, Clint Lahnen, Stephanie Mohler, Dennis Sheehan, Terri Sheehan, Chris Van Camp

MAR 2000

Contents

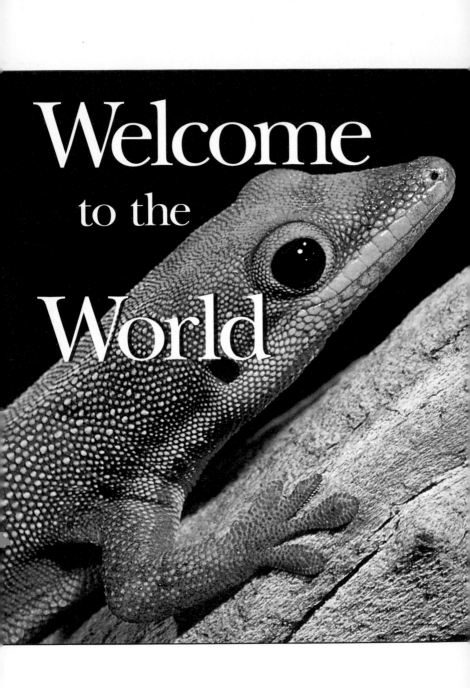

Welcome
to the
World

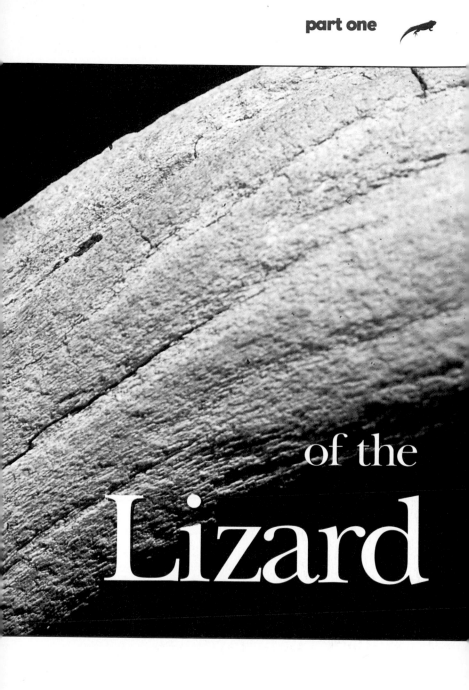

of the
Lizard

External Features of the Lizard

Parietal (Third) Eye

Snout

External Nares (Nostril)

Mouth

Eye

Dewlap

Claw

Nuchal Crest

Dorsal Crest

Thorax

Abdomen

Caudal Crest

Vent (Cloaca)

Tail

chapter 1

What Is

a Lizard?

Lizards are reptiles (class *Reptilia*) that belong to the order *Squamata,* and the suborders *Sauria* or *Lacertilia.* Snakes are also in the order *Squamata* (suborders *Serpentes* or *Ophidia*), as are an odd group of wormlike ringed or annulated reptiles known as "worm lizards"

Green Tree Monitor

(suborder *Amphisbaenia*), and lizardlike reptiles, known as the *Tuataras* or *Sphenodons* (suborder *Rhynchocephalia*), found only in New Zealand. All the creatures in the order *Squamata* are called "squamates."

Lizard Basics

Modern lizards are neither dinosaurs nor descendants of dinosaurs, even though the word "dinosaur" translates to "terrible lizard." Most lizards have elongated bodies, four legs and scaly skin and do indeed resemble dinosaurs in miniature. However, when you compare the evolution of modern lizards to that of dinosaurs, the differences between them are so great it becomes apparent that lizards are not modern day dinosaurs, in spite of their resemblance.

The majority of lizard species lay hard-shelled eggs on land. Here is a Bearded Dragon hatching.

REPRODUCTION METHODS

The majority of lizards lay hard-shelled eggs on land, although there are some that are viviparous (giving birth to live young incubated internally). One type of Brazilian skink develops its young directly in the oviduct with a placentalike link between mother and embryo, a feature unique among reptiles, although standard in mammals. Some species of lizard are all female and reproduce via a form of fertilization known as parthenogenesis, resulting in so-called "virgin-birth." No males are needed to sustain these lizard groups. However, most lizards reproduce through sexual means via internal fertilization by the male. Lizards may breed yearly, several times yearly or even every other year. Small lizards, such as geckos, may lay only one or two hard-shelled eggs (which look like pebbles); other lizards lay twenty or more eggs and some produce that many young via live birth.

Ectothermic Animals

Like all other reptiles, fish and amphibians, lizards are considered "cold-blooded." The term "cold-blooded" is actually inaccurate—when these animals are active their blood is anything but cold. A better term is "ectothermic," which means they are dependent on the temperature of their environment to warm up or cool down their bodies. Lizards thermoregulate (control their body temperatures) by basking in the sun, burrowing underground or hiding in the shade. In nature, lizards are able to control their body temperatures very precisely by seeking out different environments. In captivity, they must be given the same sorts of options—warm spots and cool spots. In order to eat, digest and metabolize their food, it is essential that they be kept warm. When resting, or if they become overheated, it is essential that they have the option of escaping the heat. This will be discussed in more detail in chapter 7.

Lizards are an extremely diverse group with over 4,000 different species and subspecies. Pictured here is a Red Flat-tailed Gecko camouflaged against the bark of a tree.

A Diverse Group

There are more than 4,000 different species and subspecies of lizards, making them among the most diverse members of the class *Reptilia*. They range in size from about 1 inch to over 10 feet in length. Several groups have absent or almost absent legs, giving these animals a snakelike appearance, although their heads are still distinctly lizardlike and they're easy to recognize as lizards. There is only one genus with two species that is truly venomous: the Helodermids, including the Gila Monster (*Heloderma suspectum*) of the southwestern United States and

> ### VENOMOUS REPTILES
>
> Unlike many snake species, very few species of lizard are venomous. Those that are venomous are not commercially traded, and you should not worry about bringing a venomous lizard into your home. Nonetheless, you should be wary of being bitten by your lizard—careful handling is the best defense.

Beaded Lizard (*Heloderma horridum*) of Mexico. There are no other venomous lizards in existence, although there are some common misconceptions that other species are also venomous. The Komodo Dragon (*Varanus komodiensis*) of Indonesia and the Bornean Earless Lizard (*Lanthanotus borneensis*) are often believed to be truly venomous due to the ferocity of their bite and the rapid infection that occurs in the wounds. People bitten by these lizards become seriously ill and may even die within days from sepsis, an infectious complication, which helps to perpetuate the myth that these lizards are venomous. Although their bites are indeed very dangerous, they are not venomous. Fortunately, none of these dangerous lizards show up in the pet trade, and they should be avoided in the unlikely event an opportunity arises to obtain one.

CONSERVATION CONSIDERATIONS

Like wildlife everywhere, lizards are threatened by habitat destruction, and their numbers are dwindling as a result of this encroachment. To help stem the loss of these fabulous animals, many species and their habitats are protected by law. Most lizards are easy to breed in captivity and ever greater numbers of lizards are supplied as pets through captive breeding programs, which helps to take pressure off wild populations heavily collected for the pet trade. In Central and South America, iguanas were not only captured for the pet trade, but also eaten and their hides used to make a variety of items. Seeing the commercial value in this popular species, government-sponsored iguana farming and ranching operations have been set up to help supply this trade and to prevent removal of free living specimens from the wild.

THREATENED SPECIES

Many lizards qualify as endangered species, although they vary in degree of endangerment. For example, all iguanas are protected under the auspices of the CITES (Convention on the International Trade of Endangered Species). This means that they may be sold in their own countries, but if these species are listed as threatened, exporting them between countries requires extensive permits. This is the reason that many iguanas bought in the United States today are bred here on "farms" or "ranches."

Like the baby turtles of the 1950s and 1960s, now banned because of the their propensity to infect small children with salmonella, baby iguanas have boomed in popularity over the past few years and may exceed the number of all other reptiles combined for the prize as the most popular reptile pet. More than one million baby iguanas are imported annually into the United States and hundreds of thousands more are brought in as unhatched fertilized eggs, which are incubated on U.S. soil for the domestic pet trade. (Unfortunately iguanas, as do most herptiles, do carry salmonella, but the threat of this infection is easy to counter with some important but simple precautions presented in chapter 9.)

Iguanas are the most popular lizard pet. (Green Iguana)

A Word to the Wise

Before anyone considers a Green Iguana or any other lizard pet, he or she has to realize that the means to house, feed and otherwise care for the lizard far exceeds the actual cost of the animal itself. This is true of tropical fish, dogs, cats and, yes, human children! To the $10 a baby iguana costs, add hundreds of dollars a year required to care for it properly. In addition to the few moments it takes for you to fall in love with the iguana at the pet store, you must commit to many hours of caring for your pet. If you are not prepared for these kinds of financial and time commitments, reconsider purchasing a pet.

Although iguanas are the most popular and among the least expensive lizard pets, there are many other interesting and unusual lizards to consider. This book will help you learn about lizards and which ones make the best pets. You will also learn how to create an ideal home environment for your lizard pet, as well as what to feed it to keep it healthy and active.

chapter 2

Anatomy
and Physiology
of Lizards

Scales

The word *squamata* is derived from the Latin word for scale, "squama." One anatomical feature all lizards share is their scaly skin—in some, soft and velvety, in others, smooth and shiny and yet in other lizards, rough, heavily armored and spiked.

Tokashiki Gecko

Lizard scales vary greatly—from small and soft or granular to large and plated. In some lizards each scale may be independent, touching others along its edges, whereas in others they overlap. Some lizards have smooth scales; others have keeled scales. A keel is a knobby protuberance from each scale. A lizard's skin has many important functions. It acts as a barrier or line of defense against microorganisms and toxic chemicals and, in the case of lizards and other reptiles, helps to conserve or prevent water loss. It can both absorb or reflect heat and some lizards change colors to enhance these properties. (Lighter skin reflects light and heat, whereas darker skin absorbs them.) The skin's many nerves receive and transmit messages about the environment to the brain, where appropriate feedback mechanisms act on such information.

All lizards have scaled skin, although the scales can vary greatly from species to species. The scales of this Blue-tongued Skink are smooth and strong.

In some lizards, such as the Horned Toad (*Phrynosoma sp.*) or Australian Thorny Devil (*Moloch sp.*), the skin has been modified into cornified spikes or horns with real defensive capabilities. In others, such as the iguana, dorsal crests and fringes of soft leathery "spikes" develop. The skin of lizards is largely devoid of glands save the femoral pores—a row of tiny holes that run partway down the ventral surface of the upper leg. These are either absent or greatly reduced in females, but are enlarged and pronounced in males. Their secretions may have several functions, including phermonal scents that attract females; in some species the waxy femoral pore secretion may aid in binding the male to the female during sexual intercourse. Not all species have obvious femoral pores. Some geckos have specialized squirting glands that are defensive in nature; the Horned Toad and Moloch are known to squirt a stream of blood out of a small pore or gland as a defensive measure. Salt glands can be found in species that find it necessary to excrete excess salt because reptiles have no sweat glands. Crusts of salt are a common sight near the nostrils of iguanids and other reptiles that excrete excess salt via these glands.

The scales of some lizards, such as the lateral fold lizards, spinytailed lizards and skinks, are reinforced by a bony plate or osteoderm—armor that makes the scales more resistant to attackers. The skin of limbed lizards also contains modified keratinous structures, known as claws, at the fingertips. These clawed finger-tips are particularly well developed in climbing species and are useful for obtaining a grip, providing self-defense and excavating or digging a nest prior to egg laying.

The most obvious aspect of a lizard's skin is its color. Some species, such as chameleons and anoles, have the spectacular ability to change the color of their skin. Skin color in lizards is controlled by structures known as chromatophores. Feedback from the ner-

vous system causes these structures to expand or shrink, resulting in color changes. There are pig-ment cells in the skin known by the color they are responsible for pro-ducing: melanophores produce blacks, browns and grays; erythrophores produce reds and xan-thophores yellows. Irido-phores contain crystals that give some species a shiny, or iridescent, appearance. Combinations of the basic chromatophores result in the greens and blues seen in many lizards. Through selective breeding, snake breeders and some gecko lizard breeders have produced entirely new colors and patterns.

The brilliant colors of this Ambanja Chame-leon are caused by chromatophores in the skin.

Some heritable mutations occur that result in the absence or near absence of all color. Animals totally devoid of pigment everywhere including the eyes (which appear red) are known as albinos. Animals not

13

totally devoid of pigment but still very pale are called leucistic. Some leucistic animals are so white they look like albinos, but the presence of pigment in the eyes is an indicator they are not true albinos. Some leucistics have been bred with unique blue or violet irises.

Skin shedding occurs because new skin is constantly being formed beneath the epidermis, which becomes worn and dried out and needs to be replaced. Although shedding may be chronologically linked with growth, shedding of the skin is not a necessary part of the growing process. It just happens to accompany it. Although all animals and even people shed their skin, none do it more spectacularly than reptiles. Snakes shed their skin in almost one entire piece. Lizards shed it in large or small patches. The process of skin shedding is known as ecdysis. Some lizards may be seen rubbing parts of their bodies against objects in their cages in order to scrape off stubborn pieces of epidermis. (Note: such scratching may also be due to external parasites, such as mites or ticks; animals that rub should be examined for these as a precaution.) A few species recycle their cast-off skin by eating it.

Nervous System

The nervous system of lizards follows the general vertebrate plan. There are organs for the five major senses: vision, hearing, feeling or touching, smelling and tasting (olfaction). There are, however, a few differences worth noting.

Vision

The eyes of lizards are adapted for day or night vision, depending on the habits of the species. In diurnal (daytime-active) lizards, vision tends to be sharp, whereas in nocturnal or burrowing animals, it is less sophisticated. Lizard eyes are, for the most part, independently operated. Their eyes, placed on the sides of the head rather than together, front forward on the face, permit little binocular vision. Binocular vision causes the brain to receive the identical image from slightly different angles and makes depth perception and precise targeting of objects in the visual path more accurate. However, having the eyes on the sides of the head allows a whole new way of looking at things. It permits lizards to see in two different directions at

once, and the peripheral vision it affords also lets lizards see what's behind them as well as what's alongside them. A few lizards, such as the true chameleons, have eyes mounted in rotating turrets. This enables chameleons to look forward, upward, downward, sideward and backward without having to tilt the head or move the body in any significant way. By focusing both eyes forward, chameleons also achieve binocular vision, helping to precisely target prey in front of them. Slight head tilts increase their visual range considerably.

DON'T EXPECT YOUR LIZARD TO PARALLEL PARK

Our eyes provide us with binocular vision, and we perceive images as a whole. Because most lizards' eyes are on opposite sides of their head, they can see what is along either side of them and even what is behind them. However, this arrangement deprives lizards of the ability to judge distances well, a trait that they share with snakes.

Most lizards have movable eyelids, but a few do not, as mentioned in the individual family or group accounts. In addition to two conventional eyes, the iguanid lizards and the tuatara have a parietal or sort of third eye located squarely on the top of the head. Also known as the median eye, it was well developed in prehistoric reptiles. If it was capable of vision in these early reptile ancestors, the parietal eye undoubtedly served to warn them of attack from above. This third eye, as it exists today, is buried beneath a layer of skin and does little but differentiate between light intensities. The parietal eye is an outgrowth of the pineal body, a glandular structure found in all vertebrate brains that is responsible for a variety of functions, including regulation of circadian rhythms (sleep/wake or rest cycles), a task aided by the ability of this accessory eye to detect light and darkness.

HEARING

All but a few lizards have fully functional ears. In some they appear as round, platelike scales or surface tympana, whereas in others the eardrum may be recessed. In general, the ears of reptiles are fairly simple. Snakes have no ears; this group depends primarily on feeling ground vibrations caused by sounds. Experiments with lizards indicate that they respond to sounds as well as low-frequency vibrations. Since only a few geckos have voices and it is not known whether they use their primitive vocal abilities to communicate, the only reason lizards would have to hear is to detect predators or prey (food).

TASTE AND SMELL

Lizard tongues not only serve as organs of taste but of odor detection as well. Lizards have a specialized organ in the roof of their mouth known as Jacobson's organ, or the vomeronasal organ. When a lizard propels its tongue into the air it picks up odor molecules and retracts them into the mouth. Once back inside the mouth, the tongue deposits these molecules onto the surfaces of the Jacobson's organ, which then translates them into olfactory information. As a rule, all reptiles have a keen and highly sensitive sense of smell. They find water and food, detect enemies or find mates using their olfactory senses. Lizards use their Jacobson's organ in addition to their normal nasal chemo-sensory receptors for odor detection.

While doing double duty as a sense organ, the tongue of many lizards is indispensable in obtaining prey. A few species also use it to wash their eyecaps. The ability of the tongue to flick out, fasten itself to a prey item and then reel it back in is nowhere so greatly developed as it is in the true chameleons. The tongue of the true chameleons is stiffened by blood sinuses that expand by pressure from the heartbeat, resulting in the tongue's rapid elongation and extensibility. Other species also use their tongue to entrap and ingest prey. The bright blue tongue of the Australian Blue-tongued Skink (*Tiliqua sp.*) is often displayed as a warning or threat to enemies, startling and scaring off many a would-be predator.

Digestive System

The digestive system of lizards begins with the mouth. Lizards have well-developed teeth. Different groups have different types, but the most common is known as pleurodont dentition. Pleurodont teeth are weakly anchored to the jaw but have elongated roots. Some types of lizards have acrodont teeth—teeth more firmly attached to the jaw—and a few types also have an inner row of top teeth on the palate in addition to regular teeth. Most insect-eating and other carnivorous lizards do not chew their prey, but simply ingest it whole. Some may attempt to break up or crush larger prey for easier handling and swallowing. Herbivorous lizards, on the other hand, tear off vegetation and appear to chew it somewhat as they swallow.

Food passes through the mouth, into the esophagus and then into the stomach, which is multichambered in some herbivorous or omnivorous species. This modification provides an area known as the hind-gut, which is used to store vegetable matter so that it can be more completely broken down and assimilated. This pro-

The incredibly quick and sticky tongue of this Parson's Chameleon enables it to capture prey easily.

cess is known as hind-gut fermentation and is accomplished by specialized bacteria.

The digestive system of lizards includes the salivary glands (to lubricate and start digestion of ingested food matter), the liver and gall bladder, the pancreas, the small and large intestines and the cloaca and anal opening or vent. Fish, amphibians, reptiles and birds are the only vertebrates with a common passageway (the cloaca) used for the excretion of liquid and sold wastes, sexual intercourse and passage of either eggs or live young into the world.

Enzymes are key chemical players in the digestion of food and they work only within a narrow range of pH and temperature, which is why temperature is so critical in reptile feeding and digestion. Below certain temperatures, many reptiles will refuse to eat and others will regurgitate rather than retain food ingested earlier at higher temperatures. Assuming one is offering food of a suitable type and size for the species involved, it is inadequate temperatures as well as physical ailments that most often are responsible for the refusal to eat in some animals. Reptiles, unlike mammals, do not have metabolisms working at a constant temperature. This is why it is critical that captives be given the opportunity to thermoregulate through a combination of appropriate air temperatures, warm spots (via heat lights or elements from above) and heating pads located beneath their substrate. In addition, overheating can stress and kill reptiles, so it is important to give them the opportunity to cool off by moving to another part of their enclosure that is not heated.

Animals with full stomachs that are not given adequate heat will not be able to digest their food. Because lizards don't readily regurgitate, the food remains in the stomach and slowly decomposes, a situation that can result in the release of fatal bacterial toxins. Because artificially hibernated captive animals will not be able to digest their food, it is necessary to withhold food for one to three weeks before hibernation to ensure that all remaining food has been digested and the residue excreted as fecal waste. (Note: Artificial hibernation is not necessary for captive reptiles that would hibernate in nature. However, it can provide a needed rest, which enables these animals to breed when they reemerge.)

Excretory System

The urinary system of lizards consists of paired kidneys intimately associated with the reproductive organs— ovaries in the females and internal testes in males. The vas deferens carry the product of the testes into the hemipenes of the lizard whereas the ureter of each kidney carries liquid or semi-solid urinary waste directly

populations and there are no males at all. This method of egg fertilization is called parthenogenesis. Since no genes are contributed by a male, the young of any given female are all identical to her, true clones of the original. Parthenogenesis is known to occur in populations of some whiptail lizards, racerunners and geckos. Biochemical changes initiate cell division and development of the embryo.

There are a few reasons why it may be important to know whether or not you have a male or female lizard. The males of some species don't get along very well, and keeping two males together in the same cage could result in fighting, with one or both lizards getting hurt in the process. And, of course, if you

---

THE ABSENT PARENT

As a rule, lizards do not make model parents by human standards. Although the mother lizard in a few species will tend to her eggs, most oviparous lizards simply deposit their eggs in a location that they believe will be adequate. Apparently a maternal instinct was not considered a necessity in the evolution of egg-laying lizards.

---

are hoping to try your hand at breeding your lizards, it is important to have a pair. Telling the difference between the sexes is easy in species that are "sexually dimorphic." This means the outward appearance of the animal can tell you whether it is a male or female. For example, male anole lizards have a flap of skin beneath the chin that is extensible and usually brightly colored; the females do not. Male fence or swift lizards may have a patch of blue color under their chins and undersides. Almost all adult, sexually mature male lizards have enlarged rows of femoral pores clearly visible on the undersides of their upper legs. This indicator can be used in sexing the common Green Iguana and many other species. If all else fails, an internal examination of the cloacal area by someone experienced will usually settle the matter.

Skeletal System

The skeletal system of lizards is also of special interest because of several unique features.

Many species, in fact members of eleven out of the fifteen families of true lizards, are capable of voluntarily breaking their tails off as a defensive measure. When confronted by a predator (including humans) a lizard's first impulse, if it can't fight, is to escape. A special arrangement in the tail vertebrae enables the lizard to tense its muscle and snap off a good part of its tail, facilitating escape. The broken-off piece of tail lies wriggling on the ground and is meant to occupy an attacker's attention while the rest of the lizard scurries off to safety. Each vertebrae of the tail has a "dotted line" called a fracture plane. When the muscles around the tail contract, a chemically mediated reaction to stress or fear, the fracture plane severs. The lizard grows a new tail, supported not by bony vertebrae but by cartilage, which is a poor replica of the original. Once a lizard uses this technique to escape it can never use it again. The voluntary breaking off of the tail is known scientifically as autotomy, a word that means self-cutting or severing.

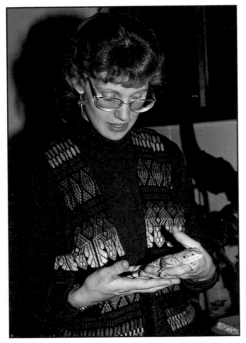

Handle your lizard carefully so you don't frighten it into autotomy in self-defense. (Clown Agama)

If you have a lizard with a perfect tail, one thing you don't want to do is mar it by causing it to commit tail autotomy. Therefore, handle such lizards carefully; never startle or grab them and never, ever pick them up by their tails or you may be left holding that part of the anatomy alone. After a lizard loses its tail, it no longer has the ability to store fat reserves, and some researchers feel tail loss impacts negatively on the animal's ability to breed and reproduce. In addition, the stump can become infected, so it's a good idea to plaster it with some antiseptic ointment as a precaution.

The rest of a lizard's skeleton is otherwise unremarkable and conforms to the standard vertebrate plan.

However, lizards, more than any other reptile pet, often suffer the consequences of a condition known as metabolic bone disease (MBD), which will be discussed in greater detail in chapter 9. MBD is prevented by making sure your lizards receive the right diet and are exposed to eight to twelve hours, or more, of UV-B light daily.

Respiratory System

The respiratory system of lizards is similar to that of all air-breathing land animals. They have two lungs and a trachea or airway, which divides into two bronchial tubes, each one feeding a lung. In most lizards the lungs are bilaterally symmetrical and well developed, but in the snakelike legless lizards the left lung is usually greatly reduced in order for it be accommodated within a narrow, cylindrical body. Reptiles do not have a diaphragm, so inhalation occurs by gulping air down and using the intercostal (between the ribs) muscles. Exhalation occurs as a passive event thanks to the elastic recoil of the lungs. Coughing and vomiting are difficult for lizards because the absence of the diaphragm does not permit them to build up the explosive pressure needed to accomplish these tasks. Lizards, turtles, snakes and crocodilians are all capable of regulating the air flow in and out of their lungs, enabling them to produce a variety of hissing sounds and body part enlargements (*e.g.* puffing up to appear bigger) as defensive gestures.

Circulatory System

All reptiles have hearts, veins, arteries and capillaries to carry blood throughout their systems. However, with the exception of the crocodilians, all reptiles including the lizards have three-, not four-chambered hearts. They have two top chambers, or right and left atria, and a single, undivided ventricle. Crocodilians, birds and mammals have four-chambered hearts by reason of a divided ventricle.

Blood is pumped by the heart throughout the body, leaving via arteries, perfusing tissues via capillary beds and returning to the right atrium via veins. From here the blood is pumped to the ventricle, and then to the lungs where it becomes reoxygenated and rids itself of excess carbon dioxide, a waste product of metabolism. The blood returns to the heart via the same ventricle, where some mixing of oxygenated and unoxygenated blood may take place. A portion of the ventricular blood is pumped back out to the body to begin the cycle once again. There is, in reality, very little mixing of arterial (oxygenated) and venous (unoxygenated) blood in the reptile's undivided ventricle, thanks to a system of channels and pressure differences that helps direct the right blood to the right place. The reptile's ability to alter its metabolic requirements because it cannot sustain a constant body temperature is an adaptation not only to unfavorable temperature conditions, but also to situations in which little oxygen is available for metabolism.

The blood of lizards contains nucleated red blood cells, a variety of white blood cells and platelets. Red blood cells (erythrocytes) carry an iron containing pigment known as hemoglobin, which binds and releases oxygen and carbon dioxide. This mechanism enables these gases to be carried to and from the tissue cells and to and from the lungs, where the excess carbon dioxide is exchanged for fresh oxygen. White blood cells are responsible for the immune responses of the organism. These cells scavenge foreign invaders and carry antibodies to destroy infectious organisms.

chapter 3

Prehistoric Origins of Lizards

The First Reptiles

Lizards and their reptile relatives, the crocodiles, snakes, tuataras and turtles, are all relics of an ancient past dating back to the upper Carboniferous Period, some 315

Mastigure

million years ago. However, the earliest reptile of all was found in Scotland, in soil dating from the lower Carboniferous Period, or 340 million years ago. This earliest known reptile was only about 8 inches long with an anapsid skull, a skull devoid of any holes other than those for the eye sockets and opening of the nasal passage. This is typical of modern turtle and tortoise skulls, but not lizards. The anapsid skull types gave rise to animals with two other distinct skull types: the synapsid and diapsid. The synapsids gave rise to the mammals. Their skull has only one opening, in the temporal region. Mammals have this single hole with a bar of bone situated within or below it. The diapsids have two holes on the sides of the skull, and include the dinosaurs and all living reptiles except the turtles and tortoises. A now extinct group of marine reptiles dating to the Mesozoic Era had just one hole situated high on the head.

The tuatara (suborder *Rhynchocephalia*) is typical of the early diapsid reptiles and is regarded as a "living fossil" for this reason. In the true lizards, the upper or temporal hole is surrounded by bone. The bar beneath the lower hole has disappeared in lizards, however.

Lizards are related to other "herps," such as snakes and turtles. (Solomon Island Skink)

The first lizards were discovered in the Triassic Period. The snakes, which appear later and are the last of the modern reptiles to have evolved, arose without doubt from the lizards. In addition to the lizards and snakes, the other and probably best known of all prehistoric diapsids were the archosaurs, or ruling reptiles: the dinosaurs. Their ascendancy marks the start of the Age of the Ruling Reptiles in the Permian Period, some 280 to 230 million years ago, which lasted throughout the Mesozoic Era, up to 225 million years ago. The Mesozoic Era most assuredly belonged to these ruling reptiles—dinosaurs and their relatives, the crocodilians and flying reptiles, or pterosaurs. The dinosaurs' extinction around the end of the Cretaceous Period, some 65 million years ago, paved the way for the rise of the mammals, and eventually man. Whatever killed these giant reptiles spared smaller animals, including reptiles and mammals, which evolved into the animal forms alive today.

Reptiles Diverge

The oldest discovered diapsid, about 300 million years old (from the upper Carboniferous Period), was found in the U.S. It measured 16 inches in length, and judging from its teeth and gape, was probably an insect eater. The diapsids divided into two different groups: the archosaurs (dinosaurs, crocodilians and pterosaurs) and the Lepidosauromorphs, which included the lizards, worm lizards, tuataras and snakes. It is generally agreed that lizards, specifically the worm lizards, are the snake's closest relative and immediate ancestor.

Lizards have everything that snakes lack—ears so they can hear, eyelids so they can blink and, of course, four legs. The fossorial or burrowing limbless lizards, some of which survive today, are halfway to becoming snakes, and it is these limbless lizards from which the snakes clearly evolved.

Lizards share some obvious characteristics with the dinosaurs, but they are not descended from the extinct animals. (Solomon Island Skink)

While lizards and dinosaurs were both diapsids, the skeletal features of the lizards and other squamates differ so greatly from the dinosaurs it is not considered possible that modern lizards descended in any way from the ruling reptiles. The fact that the dinosaurs became extinct 65 million years ago indicates that the lizards continued to evolve separately from their dead reptile cousins. Only one archosaur survived the great dinosaur extinction—the crocodilians. These advanced amphibious reptiles with four-chambered hearts in no way resemble modern lizards, except in outward appearance. In fact, crocodilians are believed to be more closely related to birds than they are to the other reptiles.

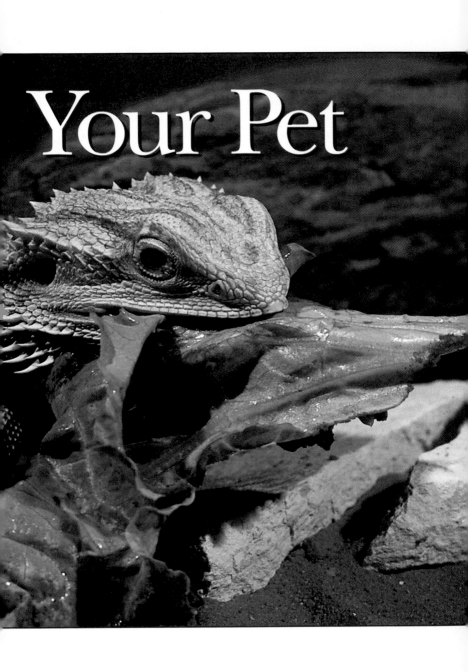

Your Pet

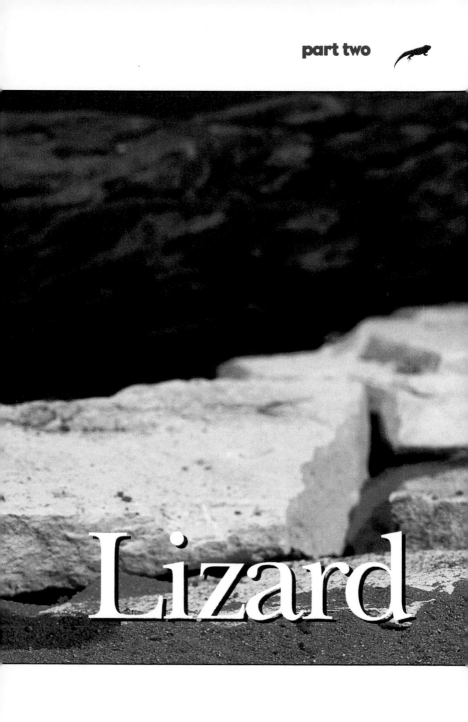

part two

Lizard

chapter 4

Why a Reptile Pet?

Gold Dust Day Gecko

The title "pet" for reptiles is misleading, as animals such as lizards are not cuddly creatures that exactly fit the traditional notion of a "pet." Lizards are wild creatures that will never become as acculturated to humans as dogs, cats, horses or even Asian elephants. There are other reasons for choosing to acquire, care for and even try to breed an animal such as a lizard.

A Piece of the Wild World

More than twenty years ago, on New York's upper east side, there was a small store called "A Small World," or something similar. It was a wondrous place, and it was way before its time. It closed, and the enthusiastic and knowledgeable owner who was always so willing to share information with you, even if you didn't buy anything, disappeared along with the shop. New York has never seen another place like it. What was this magical place? For want of a better description, it was a reptile store or a terrarium shop.

It was filled with lovingly tended and expertly constructed miniature dioramas. Each of the setups was a piece of the great outdoors, housing not only mosses, plants, vines and tiny ponds, but also a variety of small frogs or lizards. There were working real-life models of deserts, scrublands, tropical rain forests and other natural habitats, crafted in miniature. The art of terrarium building and maintenance never really became popular in America, but in many European countries this hobby is on a par with fish- or birdkeeping.

Pet reptiles allow us to have a piece of remote and exotic places. (Texas Collared Lizard)

What compels people to pursue the keeping of exotic wild creatures and to erect miniature versions of their faraway homes? This question has a simple answer as well as a complex one. The simple answer lies in the fascination with the unfamiliar and the exotic—every child's fascination with, and desire to learn more about, the world beyond his or her horizon. But what happens when that child grows up? What then continues to spark enthusiasm for this hobby? One contributing factor is certainly every human's love of the world and the living things within it, and the innate desire to somehow connect with the otherwise unattainable parts of this world. In other words, since it may not be possible for many of us to trek through Brazil's Amazon, the next best thing is to bring a piece of that world into our own.

An Educational Hobby

There are other reasons for choosing living reptiles as a pastime or hobby. There are few hobbies as educational or broadening, at least in a scientific, biological and geographic sense, as the study of reptiles and amphibians. Parents should recognize the educational value of such a hobby and encourage it. And adults who never had the chance to pursue an education on this level can access a vast body of printed and on-line (Internet) information on every imaginable aspect of these animals, including, but not limited to, biogeography, ecology, anatomy and physiology, life history and reproduction, pathology, conservation and numerous other disciplines that interface with one's interest in herps (reptiles and amphibians). Educational opportunities for herpetophiles are numerous and popular. You can attend a monthly lecture at your local herp society, subscribe to one or more popular herp magazines or scientific journals and add a new book to your reptile library. And while reptiles will never eclipse dogs, cats or birds as animals in the home, there are millions of U.S. and overseas households where the whole family has found a common interest in herps and the opportunity to observe, study and learn more together.

Learning about lizards is a rewarding hobby. (Wonder Gecko)

Why a Lizard?

But why a lizard rather than another reptile? In addition to lizards there are snakes, turtles and tortoises and crocodilians to consider. Each, however, has its pros and cons as a pet. Crocodilians make poor animals for keeping in the home because of their unruly temperaments and specialized housing needs, linked mainly to their large size and amphibious requirements. So while some brave people have adopted a crocodilian such as an alligator, caiman or crocodile, the commitment of time, space and money may be too much for others.

Turtles and tortoises make excellent pets, but turtles often require a fully aquatic or semiaquatic environment. This means substantial investments of time and money to maintain a hygienic environment in which in the animals can thrive.

Snakes are fairly easy to maintain, but there are some problems with them, too. Venomous species should definitely be ruled-out, as should large snakes such as pythons, unless you have substantial space and facilities to cage and care for them safely and adequately. In addition there is always a family member, whether it's Aunt Tillie over for a visit or Grandpa who lives in the apartment upstairs, who has a genuine, psychological fear of snakes (called ophidophobia by psychologists). Phobias should be taken quite seriously; if someone in your household is phobic of snakes, it is best to respect his or her fear. The stress of some phobias is enough to cause ulcers, heart attacks and high blood pressure. In addition, snakes, for the most part, eat mice or rats, either dead or alive, so some people consider feeding them rather unpleasant.

Although many people are afraid of snakes, few will mind lizards like this Giant Day Gecko.

This leaves lizards—everyone's favorite. Phobia of lizards is extremely rare; chances are no one in your family will mind living with these creatures. Many lizards are vegetarians, and the majority of smaller carnivorous lizards eat mainly insects. Generally, people feel that feeding insects to their pets is less objectionable

33

than feeding them rodents. Of course some larger lizards such as the monitors would also relish a rodent meal, but amazingly many of these can be fed cooked meats, chicken and hard-boiled eggs, much the same sort of stuff we ourselves eat. So the lizards win claws down!

A LIZARD IS A WILD ANIMAL

Remember at all times that your lizard, although a wonderful pet, is nonetheless a wild animal. Through companionship and gentle handling, a lizard can be tamed. However, no lizard can be domesticated in the same fashion as a dog or a cat. Expect the unexpected from your lizard and you will have a good understanding of your pet.

Taming Your Lizard

Lizards *can* be conditioned to remain calm in the face of human interaction once they learn their humans have no intention of harming them. However, it is a serious mistake to dress them up in leather jackets, hats or sunglasses, or put them on leashes and take them for walks, even though pet industry manufacturers are making such gear. Harnesses and other articles of clothing can damage the lizard's skin. In iguanas, especially, equipment like this has been implicated in the destruction of their dorsal crests or spikes, causing abscesses and other cutaneous (skin) infections.

This Egyptian Mastigure is a long-term captive. Although its claws are long and sharp, years of gentle handling ensure that it won't scratch its handler.

Lizards are not domestic animals such as horses, dogs or cats and become tame only by a type of learning known as conditioning, which is also used with domesticated animals. However, as nondomestic species, lizards and other wild animals may be more unpredictable with respect to behavior and cannot be trusted as one would trust a well-trained dog or horse. In addition, many lizards, when picked up by humans (or anything larger than they are), engage in a natural behavior known as thanatosis, or freezing. Technically the word means "death feigning." By feigning death, animals in the wild often can escape attack by a predator. The animal, realizing it is no use to fight, simply stands stock still. Many lizards engage in this type of natural behavior, which is mistakenly attributed to their being tame. This does not, however, mean that lizards cannot be conditioned by frequent handling, learning that the process is of no threat to them.

The best way to condition your lizard is through frequent handling. Some lizards may be jumpy and scratch or try to bite and get away. These have to be handled cautiously, if at all, and it takes much work to quiet them down. Some lizard species are so naturally skittish that they never calm down and are often considered "untamable."

> **JOIN YOUR LOCAL HERPETOLOGICAL SOCIETY**
>
> Enhance the educational value of your pet lizard by joining a local herpetological society. These groups will conduct seminars and provide literature on all aspects of lizard care. Other experienced lizard owners can share their tips with you. Best of all, many societies work to ensure the safety of lizards in their natural environment—by getting involved you can learn about lizards and help to protect them at the same time.

Large-clawed lizards such as monitors or bigger iguanids can inflict serious injuries, and it is not unusual for them to draw blood. Such wounds should be washed out with soap and hot water and disinfected thoroughly. To minimize scratching and biting, large, skittish lizards must be picked up and handled by holding one hand gently but firmly around the back of the neck and the other around the middle body, keeping the legs tucked into the sides of the body. Wear heavy clothing, long sleeves and work gloves to help prevent scratch or bite injuries.

If you start off with a fairly docile species, and interact with your lizard regularly, chances are it will reward you with a calm and unfrightened demeanor when you hold it.

chapter 5

Lizard
Families

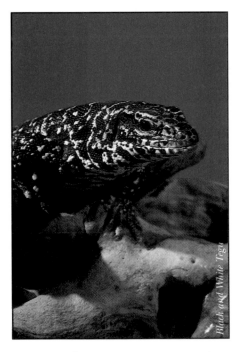

Black and White Tegu

Lizards, like other animals, have both common and scientific names. For example, the Common Green Anole's scientific name is *Anolis carolinenesis*. *Anolis* refers to the genus and *carolinenesis* to the specific species. The scientific name is usually derived from either Latin or Greek, and is in two parts for species and three parts for subspecies. When discussing a whole group of lizards from a single genus, only the first part of the name will be used. Example: Anoles (*Anolis sp.*); "sp." includes all the species in that genus. There are sixteen families of lizards.

Lizard Families

FAMILY AGAMIDAE—AGAMA OR CHISEL-TOOTHED LIZARDS

The agama lizards are found throughout Africa, Asia and Australia. They range in size from 2½ to 6 inches, not including the tail. There are a few exceptional variants, such as the tiny (½ inch) Australian Small-scaled Lizard (*Amphibolorus microlepidotus*), and the giant Sail-fin Water Dragon (*Hydrosaurus amboinensis*) with a body nearly 2 feet long, and with the tail, nearly 4 feet total. There are more than 300 species of agamid lizard. Agamids are primarily insect eaters, but some larger forms will eat bird and reptile eggs, and the spiny-tailed lizards or mastigures (*Uromastyx sp.*) are primarily vegetarians or herbivores.

Agamids are, for the most part, abroad in the daylight and have well-developed vision and hearing to help protect them from predators. The Australian Frilled Dragon (*Chlamydosaurus kingii*) escapes its enemies by standing erect on its hind legs and racing away at break-neck speed. Other agamids, known as the flying dragons (*Draco sp.*), can fly (actually glide) from tree limb to tree limb. These Asian lizards have a large, thin flap of skin that extends from each side of the body between the front and rear limbs. When this parachutelike structure is fully spread, it is supported by six to eight bony ribs. As the animal glides it uses its tail as a rudder, steering it to a desired landing spot. While the flying dragons have flight adaptations, the water dragons (*Hydrosaurus sp.*), have broad, oarlike tails that are used to propel them through water.

Agamids, like this Russian Big-mouth Agamid, have well-developed hearing and eye-sight to protect them from predators.

The majority of agamids are egg layers, depositing anywhere from one to twenty-five eggs per clutch. However, there are two groups that give birth to live young: the Sri Lankan Prehensile-tailed Lizards and the Toad-headed Lizards (*Phrynocephalus sp.*) of the Middle East. Many lizards from this family are available as pets.

Although difficult to keep in captivity, true chameleons, like this Panther Chameleon, offer a host of rewards for the experienced hobbyist.

FAMILY CHAMELEONIDAE—TRUE (OLD-WORLD) CHAMELEONS

The old-world or true chameleons should not be confused with the small lizards known popularly in the United States as chameleons. The U.S. chameleons are really a type of iguanid lizard known as an anole. They are called chameleons because of their ability to change color between green and brown, but the true chameleon's color-changing ability leaves these anole lizards far behind. In addition to the familiar green and brown shades, true chameleons sport blues, reds, yellows and can even be induced to change their patterns.

True chameleons are among the most remarkable, spectacular and unusual lizards in the world. Many dedicated fanciers have devoted their lives to developing specialized conditions for keeping, breeding and rearing these lizards. The true chameleons are found primarily in Africa and on the island of Madagascar.

These lizards are not for the novice, but experienced lizard keepers will find them a rewarding challenge.

True chameleons range in size from the dwarf chameleons (*Bradypodion sp.*) of South Africa, with a body length of 2½ to 5 inches, to the Madagascan leaf chameleons (*Brooksia sp.*), with body lengths rarely reaching 2 inches to chameleons of the genus *Chameleo,* which are among the most wide-ranging and largest species, some having body lengths of 1 foot or more.

Among the more remarkable features of the true chameleons are their specialized feet. Their toes point in two different directions, enabling them to grab onto and walk on slim branches and vines. They also have prehensile tails to grab branches and help them maintain balance. Their narrow, flattened bodies are well adapted for walking slim vines and branches; their body shape helps distribute their weight on such walkways. Their turreted eyes work both binocularly and independently of each other.

Their unusually precise vision and long sticky tongues, which they can thrust out at lightening speeds, enable chameleons to target and retrieve tasty insects before the prey can react. Although some species may move along the ground, most of the true chameleons are tree dwellers (arboreal) and rarely descend, except to deposit their eggs.

Chameleons have been termed "masters of disguise" and use their unique color changing ability, known scientifically as metachrosis, to escape detection by enemies. They can blend into almost any background. Their slow, deliberate gait and frozen stance also protect them against predation and help them to capture prey, fast-moving insects that would flee in an instant if the chameleon's presence were revealed.

FAMILY IGUANIDAE—IGUANID LIZARDS

Iguanas are found throughout North, Central and South America, in the West Indies, in the South Pacific, including on the Galapagos Islands and Fiji

Although not as popular a pet as the Green Iguana, this Rhino Iguana is also a member of the iguanid family.

and on the island of Madagascar. There are more than 900 species of iguanid lizards worldwide, and they've adapted to every conceivable habitat, including in or near salt water, brackish water and fresh water. There are iguanids that live in trees and others that scamper along the ground. One type of iguanid, the Basilisk Lizard (*Basilicus basilicus*), is also known as the Jesus Christ Lizard because its favorite mode of escape is to walk (actually run) on water. It stands erect on its two hind legs, spreads it toes and takes off across the surface, leaving bewildered enemies or predators behind on the shore. Basilisk Lizards are frequently available as pets. Some types of iguanas live in arid deserts, others in humid rain forests or tropical jungles. The famed Marine Iguanas (*Amblyrhynchus cristatus*) of the Galapagos Islands are among the most extraordinary members of this group, living on sparse rocky outcroppings and diving into the ocean to forage for algal seaweed. All iguanas are primarily herbivorous (vegetarian), but a few will take animal protein as part of their diet. The common Green Iguana (*Iguana iguana*) is a strict vegetarian and needs a varied diet of vitamin and mineral rich foods to sustain it in captivity.

Iguanas range in size from only a few inches to 6 feet or more, including their tails. Colors are predominantly green, brown or grayish-black. The Marine Iguana develops brightly colored irregularly shaped patches of red. The Fiji Iguana looks very much like the common Green Iguana, except that it is barred with white stripes. It is not available in the pet trade because it is strictly protected as an endangered species, as are the Marine Iguanas and numerous other species of these spectacular lizards.

Among the North American iguanids frequently available as pets are the collared lizards (*Crotaphytes sp.*); the pancakelike, spiked little lizard known erroneously as the "horned toad" (*Phrynosoma sp.*) and the fence lizards or swifts (*Sceloporus sp.*), of which there are fifty or more species and subspecies. There are many excellent pet candidates among the iguanids.

Unlike their cousins, the true geckos, eyelid geckos, like this Lichtenfeld's Eyelid Gecko, have eyelids that can open and shut.

FAMILY EUBLEPHARIDAE—THE EYELID OR LEOPARD GECKOS

This small group of gecko lizards has only six genera (plural of genus) and about two dozen species. As their name implies, they have true eyelids. One genus is arboreal, but the rest are ground dwellers. They are found in some parts of Africa, in southwest Asia and in the southwest United States into Central America. They favor arid or semiarid (scrub) habitats

THE LEOPARD GECKO'S DIET

An insectivore, the Leopard Gecko will eat crickets, grasshoppers and flies. A Leopard Gecko in the wild may even catch and eat a smaller lizard. Because they can store excess food in their tails, they prefer not to shed their tails as a defense mechanism.

and lay only two eggs at a time. They are popular with gecko aficionados.

FAMILY GEKKONIDAE—TRUE GECKOS AND THE LEGLESS LIZARDS

This family contains all of the geckos except the eyelid geckos. The true geckos differ from the eyelid geckos

41

by having fused, immovable eyelids. They protect their eyes with a clear spectacle or lenslike piece of skin. (In fact, reptiles' spectacles, or eyecaps, helped to inspire the invention of the contact lens.) The eyecap is shed along with the rest of the animal's skin on a periodic basis. There are some 900 or more species and sub-species in some eighty genera. They are extremely successful in their ability to colonize new territory. They inhabit every continent except Antarctica, and are also found on many oceanic islands. Geckos thrive in temperate and tropical climates and are absent from more northerly ranges. Many species of gecko adapt well to living near or in human housing. It is not unusual to see these small lizards on the interior as well as exterior walls of houses, where they find insects to eat.

They range in size from the miniature Least Gecko (*Sphaerodactylus sp.*), with a body length (excluding tail) of a mere ½ inch, to the giant geckos of Australia and New Caledonia (*Rhacodactylus sp.*), some of which reach body lengths, excluding tail, of 10 inches or more. Some species of gecko come out only at night (nocturnal), whereas others are strictly day prowlers (diurnal); a few species are active around dawn and/or dusk.

American soldiers in Vietnam believed they heard people speaking in the forest around them; however, these sounds were most likely made by Tokay Geckos.

While most geckos conform to the standard tetrapod (four-legged) form, a few types are nearly legless and look more like snakes than lizards. If you look carefully with a small magnifier you can see tiny, just about useless legs. One Australian group, the *Pygopoda,* have no front limbs whatsoever and nothing more than a small scaly flap for rear legs. The legless geckos are semifossorial (burrowing), seeking shelter beneath the ground during the day and going out at night to forage. You can easily distinguish legless lizards from snakes by looking carefully at the head region. Lizards have ear holes and more angular heads, whereas snakes have a torpedolike profile.

Arboreal or climbing geckos are noted for their amazing foot pads that enable them to adhere to the sides of walls or branches, even smooth glass, as if they were pasted on, but no glue is involved. Their prodigious climbing and wall-walking abilities are based solely on frictional adhesion.

Geckos lay only one or two eggs per clutch and most are easy to breed and hatch out. Geckos make excellent study examples and vivarium pets, although a few of the larger species, such as the Tokay Gecko (*Gekko gecko*) of southeast Asia, tend to be rather nasty and their bite can draw blood. The bite of smaller species is nothing more than a nip.

Although most lizards are basically mute and can make only an occasional hiss, members of the gecko family make a variety of sounds, such as clicks, some of which actually resemble words to the human ear. This is because of their unusually well-developed vocal cords. During the Vietnam War, U.S. troops often thought they heard voices from the forest screaming curses in English toward them. These sounds were most likely made by Tokay Geckos, not the Viet Cong as they believed.

Family Anguidae—The Lateral Fold Lizards

The anguid, or lateral fold, lizards are widely distributed in Europe, and have representatives along the west coast of the U.S. and throughout the southeastern U.S. into Texas, Mexico and Central America to the northern coast of South America. They are absent through mid–South America, but are found again in southeastern South America.

These fast-moving little lizards are popular and interesting pets. They range in shape from short and tubby to long and slender. Some species have limbs, some have greatly reduced limbs and others, such as the Slow Worm (*Anguis frailis*), have no limbs at all. A few live in trees, navigating with the help of a prehensile tail, although most anguids are either ground dwellers or burrowers. They can be found in a variety of temperate and hot climates and in conditions ranging from arid to very wet.

Glass Lizards are lizards, although they may look like snakes at first glance.

Larger anguids eat small birds, lizards or mice, whereas smaller ones are content to feed on tadpoles, earthworms, spiders, crickets, grasshoppers and other bugs. A legless type, known as the Sheltopusik or Balkan Glass Lizard (*Ophiosaurus apodus*), eats slugs and snails. European farmers welcome the presence of this lizard as a natural predator of these crop pests. Two of the most familiar anguid lizards available as pets are the Eastern Alligator Lizard (*Gerrhontus sp.*) and the Western Alligator Lizard (*Elgaria sp.*) of the U.S. The legless Glass Lizards (*Ophio-saurus sp.*) are also popular.

Anguids range in size from the tiny Pygmy Alligator Lizard (*Elgaria parva*), with a body length of 2½ inches, to the snakelike Sheltopusik (*Ophiosaurus apodus*) mentioned above, with a body length of nearly 2 feet. If you include the tail, this lizard has a maximum length of nearly 5 feet!

FAMILY CORDYLIDAE—SPINYTAILED LIZARDS

The spinytailed or armored lizards are found in sub-Saharan Africa and on the island of Madagascar. They range in size from a few inches to some 2 feet in length. Most of these lizards live in arid environments, scrubland or forests. Their water-conserving abilities enable some populations to survive on rocky barrens devoid of water and with little rainfall.

Most are omnivorous (eating both plant and animal matter). All are egg layers save one group, the *Cordylines,* which give birth to one to six live young annually. Egg layers produce between four and five eggs per clutch. The flat lizards (*Platysaurus sp.*) lay only two extremely elongated eggs in rocky crevices.

Members of the genus cordylus, like this Sungazer, are among the more popular spinytailed lizards in the pet trade.

These interesting and strange looking lizards become available from time to time as pets, particularly members of the wide ranging genera *Cordylus* (spinytailed lizards) and *Gerrhosaurus* (plated lizards).

FAMILY DIBAMIDAE—BLIND LIZARDS

The blind lizards are small, snakelike (nearly limbless) lizards found in Indonesia, Malaysia and in one small pocket extending between Mexico and Texas on the Gulf of Mexico. Size range is between 2 and 7 inches.

There are just twelve species of blind lizard and they are all burrowing or fossorial with tiny eyes situated underneath scale flaps. They are essentially sightless and rely on other senses to navigate, feed and reproduce. The front legs and pectoral bones are absent entirely and all that remain of the rear legs are tiny scale flaps. They burrow in forested regions into moist soils. One species, the Mexican Blind Lizard (*Anelytropis papillosus*), is adapted to arid or drier regions. Their mode of reproduction is not known, but it is believed that they incubate their eggs internally.

Diet consists of small, ground-dwelling bugs and perhaps slugs. They are not a good choice for a lizard pet because of difficulty finding appropriate foods and their shy and reclusive nature.

FAMILY GYMNOPHTHALMIDAE— MINIATURE OR SPECTACLED TEGUS

These small, often brightly colored, common lizards are found in southern Mexico and throughout Central and South America, except along most of the Pacific Coast. There are more than 120 species.

They are primarily ground dwellers, resting just beneath the surface where they eat a variety of insects and grubs. The genus *Gymnophthalmus* is known to contain bisexual members and is one of the few lizard groups capable of unisexual reproduction.

They are often available as pets, are easy to feed and make colorful and interesting additions to a properly outfitted terrarium.

They should not be confused with the true tegu lizards, a group of much larger-sized lizards (see below). At one time they were thought to be miniature versions of the tegus, but they do not look anything like the tegus and have appropriately been assigned a separate family of their own.

FAMILY HELODERMATIDAE—GILA MONSTERS AND BEADED LIZARDS

This family of lizards consists of just two species, the Gila Monster of the American southwest (*Heloderma suspectum*) and the Mexican Beaded Lizard (*Heloderma horridum*). There are also several subspecies of these species based on geographic range and color and pattern differences. These are the only true venomous lizards in the world. However, their venom apparatus differs markedly from that of the venomous snakes. While snakes have venom glands at the rear of their upper jaws, helodermid venom glands are situated on each side of the rear lower jaw. Snake venom glands have a singe delivery duct, whereas helodermid glands are multiducted, with a delivery vessel carrying venom from each lobe of the multilobed gland. Venom is delivered not by fangs, but by grooved teeth that chew the venom into the victim.

The Gila Monster is one of two poisonous lizards. Both poisonous lizards belong to the family Helodermatidae.

While shy and reclusive in nature, captives that become startled or threatened will attack ferociously with sharp teeth, hanging on to their victims in a manner some observers (and victims) say seems more like a Pit Bull Terrier than a lizard. If cornered or threatened, these lizards will attack, so if you are lucky enough to happen on to one in the wild, give it wide berth.

Clearly, these lizards are not suitable as pets. While their venom is rarely fatal, it causes excruciating pain and swelling. Because bites are rare and almost never fatal to humans, there is no commercially available antivenom. Deaths in animals bitten by helodermids are due to cardiac arrest and/or shock.

FAMILY LACERTIDAE—TRUE, WALL OR SAND LIZARDS

This large (over 200 species) family of common lizards is found throughout Europe, Asia (including Japan and Korea), the Middle East and Africa.

Lacertids are probably the most commonly seen lizards in Europe. They sport a wide variety of colors and patterns. The European Jeweled Lacerta (*Lacerta lepidus*) and the Emerald Lacerta (*Lacerta viridis*) are commonly available, as are a number of other members of this lizard family.

Lacertids rarely exceed 8 inches in length. They have long tails, typical lizard bodies and four fully functional legs. Most are insectivores, eating small bugs and grubs. One species (*Aporosaura anchietae*), found in Southern Africa's harsh Namib Desert, eats seeds. Lacerta are primarily ground dwellers, foraging in low lying vegetation or bushes. Only one species is arboreal: the Sawtailed Lizard (*Holaspis guentheri*), which flattens its entire body to serve as a wing or aerofoil when gliding from branch to branch. Lacertids have large eyes with movable eyelids, and some species have a remarkable transparent window in the lower lid, which enables them to see with their lids closed.

THE LIZARD'S PLACE IN THE REPTILE WORLD

Reptiles get their name from the Latin word reptilia, which means "to crawl." The order Squamata, is shared by lizards (suborder Sauria) with snakes (suborder Serpentes). Other reptile orders are the Chelonia (turtles and tortoises); the Rhyncocephalia, consisting of one extant member, the lizardlike Tuatara; and the Amphisbaenids, wormlike animals that live underground.

Many lacertids make excellent pets. They're easy to feed, have undemanding requirements and are fairly long-lived if cared for properly. One species is recorded to have lived twenty years in captivity.

Lacertids, like this European Jeweled Lacerta, make excellent pets.

FAMILY SCINIDAE—SKINKS

There are approximately a thousand different species of skink worldwide—throughout North, Central and South America and in Africa, Europe, Eastern Europe, Asia, Indo-Malaysia and the Australian archipelago, as well as on many oceanic islands throughout the world. They are a highly successful and diversified group of lizards. They occupy every conceivable habitat and climate, including near salt water and fresh water; they are even found as high as the tree line of the Himalayan mountains. They are primarily ground dwellers and burrowers, although some are at least semiarboreal and a few are semiaquatic as well. Most ground-dwelling or terrestrial skinks are semifossorial. They range in size from 1 inch to as long as 15 inches or more in body length, longer if you count the tail. They are noted for their flat, shiny scales and cylindrical bodies.

One of the largest and most popular skinks kept as pets is the Blue-tongued Skink (*Tilaquia sp.*), some species of which are heavy bodied and measure 1½ feet or more in length when fully grown, including their tail.

Blue-tongued Skinks are also found in Australia but their export is prohibited, so most legally imported Blue-tongued Skinks seen in the pet trade are from Indonesia. Yes, they do have a brightly colored blue tongue, which is a sight to behold. They use their tongue as a warning or defensive gesture to ward off enemies as well as to help secure prey.

The majority of skinks have four well-developed limbs, but a few species have severely reduced limbs, which forces them to resort to a more snakelike form of loco-motion. Some skinks are completely limbless.

Blue-tongued Skinks brandish their tongues as defensive or warning gestures.

Some skinks lay few eggs, as few as one and rarely more than three of four. Others give birth to live young and still other species are ovoviviparous, which means they produce eggs but incubate them internally.

FAMILY TEIIDAE—THE TEGU LIZARDS

The tegu lizards, also known as racerunners and whip-tails, include some 240 species. They are found in the southern United States and in Mexico, Central America and throughout most of South America, save the southernmost tip. Teiids also occur in the West Indies. Most teiids are only about 5 or 6 inches long, but a few grow much longer, with body lengths of 20 inches or more. Almost all have well-developed limbs on a sturdy body. They have movable eyelids, often cov-ered with scales.

They are primarily ground-dwelling lizards and are found in a diverse number of habitats ranging from arid to wet, from scrublands to rain forest. They are egg layers and one genus, *Cnemidophorous,* or the whip-tails, reproduces unisexually by parthenogenesis as well as sexually. Teiids are active during the day when temperatures are high. Their diet ranges from insects and grubs in the smaller species to birds, small mammals and eggs in the larger species. One group, the Caiman Lizards, subsists primarily on snails, the shells of which they crack open with their powerful teeth and jaws.

Many tegus, like this juvenile Black and White South American Lizard, have long been popular as pets.

Larger teiids, such as the common Black and White South American Lizard, and Red and Black and Gold and Black variants of this genus (*Tupinambis sp.*), have long been popular as pets. Other teiid lizards seen frequently as pets include ameivas (*Ameiva sp.*), Caiman Lizards, racerunners and whiptails of the arid American southwest.

FAMILY VARANIDAE—THE MONITOR LIZARDS

The monitor lizards are among the most spectacular of all the lizard groups. They range in size from the small Australian Desert Monitor, known as the Pygmy Goanna (*Varanus brevicauda*), which measures less than 6 inches, to the giant Komodo Island (Indonesia) Monitor, which measures 10 feet including its tail and weighs 500 or more pounds.

The common name monitor lizard is thought to derive from the fact that many of these lizards would scavenge off prey at the water's edge and would flee at the approach of crocodiles also in search of a meal. When they took off it was a signal for people in the area to get out of harm's way as well. Thus they were "monitoring," or warning of the approach of these dangerous creatures. Another theory claims that the name derives from some monitors' curious habit of standing erect on their hind limbs, peering over hedges or rocks to survey the approach of an enemy or possible food source, "monitoring" the situation around them. Australians call their monitor lizards "goannas," a spin on the word "iguana." Although monitors are not members of the iguana lizard family, the traditional Australian name predates the nomenclatural precision of today.

The Savannah Monitor is a popular pet.

Monitors are found throughout Africa (except in the northern deserts), throughout the Middle East, India, southern Asia, Indo-Malaysia, through Papua New Guinea and down through most of Australia. There are about thirty-five species, many of which regularly show up in the pet trade. They have small heads, long necks, stout bodies and sturdy limbs.

All monitors are carnivores and voracious predators, although one Philippine species, Gray's Monitor (*Varanus olivaceus*), is known to eat fruit. Smaller species prey on insects, frogs, fish, small reptiles and mammals. The larger the lizard, the larger the prey. The Komodo Island Monitors (found also on the islands of Flores and Padar) are known to bring down and feed on goats, deer and free roaming calves.

Because almost all monitors also scavenge dead prey, they can be encouraged in captivity to eat pre-killed foods such as chicken, beef, canned dog food and other store-bought meats and animal chows.

Among the most popular monitor lizards seen for sale in the pet trade are the Nile Monitor (*Varanus niloticus*), the Savannah Monitor (*Varanus exanthematicus*) and the Water Monitor (*Varanus salvator*). Other popular species include the Peach Throated Monitor (*Varanus jobiensis*) and the White Throated Monitor (*Varanus albigularis*). The rare and endangered Bornean Earless Monitor Lizard (*Lathanotus borneensis*) is the sole member of its genus but is included in the monitor family, although at one time it was believed to be more closely related to the venomous lizard family *Helodermatidae*. It is not commercially available because of its endangered species status and, in any case, makes a poor choice for a pet—its bite is notoriously infective.

Although a number of species forage near water and may enter from time to time, only one species regularly feeds, rests and hides underwater: Merten's Water Monitor (*Varanus mertensi*).

FAMILY XANTUSIIDAE—THE NIGHT LIZARDS

This is a small group (about twenty species) of small lizards found from the southwestern U.S. through Central America and in eastern Cuba. They have immovable eyelids that form eyecaps and, like other lizards with such an arrangement, perform the remarkable chore of cleaning debris away from their eyecaps by using their tongues.

These lizards are primarily abroad in the day, although they are shy and scurry about under the cover of leaf litter and other forest floor debris. The fact that they are never seen in the day led to the erroneous common name of "night lizards," which has stuck with them in spite of evidence that they are not nocturnal.

The Central American species live in lowland forests. The southwestern U.S. forms have adapted to life in the arid deserts and scrublands of the region. They eat about anything they can swallow and are omnivorous, consuming both plant as well as animal matter.

They are all live bearers, producing only a few young annually or every two years. Unisexual as well as bisexual populations are known to exist.

FAMILY XENOSAURIDAE—KNOB SCALED LIZARDS

The *Xenosauridae,* or knob scaled lizards, are a small family of four species, three found in Mexico south to Guatamala and one, the Crocodile Lizard (*Shinisaurus crocodilurus*), found in southern China. They get their common name from the fact that their dorsal (back) region scales are heavily armored with rows of knob-like projections. These lizards occur in moist, semi-moist as well as dry scrubland environments. The Chinese Crocodile Lizard is semiaquatic, entering the water to feed on fish and other aquatic organisms. These lizards may grow up to 16 inches in length, including the tail, and are relatively heavy bodied. They have sharp, fang-like, cutting teeth and can inflict a painful wound when they bite. Local Chinese myths say the Crocodile Lizard is venomous, which it isn't, though its tiny red eyes lend credence to the belief.

All members of this family give birth to live young. They are rarely offered as pets and are subject to international treaties that regulate their trade. Captive-bred and -reared Crocodile Lizards are available from time to time, but their prices remain high.

chapter 6

Choosing
a Pet
Lizard

With some 4,000 or so different species of lizard, how does one decide which lizard or lizards to choose? You don't have to worry too much about that, as over 3,500 of all the world's lizards are almost never available in the pet trade. It is safe to say there are only about 100 to 150 different lizard species that are ever com-

Bearded Dragon (golden phase)

mercially available, and you would have to look far and wide to even find that many different kinds to choose from. The average mail-order or dedicated reptile business usually has no more than twenty different kinds of lizards at any one time, sometimes far fewer.

There are many factors to consider when making a rational decision about choosing a lizard. Unfortunately many people decide which lizard to get based on impulse, and this can be a bad idea.

Important Factors in Making Your Choice

Now that you've decided to get a lizard, which one should you choose and why? The first and foremost consideration, aside from price, is the size to which your lizard will grow and the space that it needs. If your space is limited, you should start off with a lizard you can comfortably accommodate in your own living quarters. Baby iguanas may be inexpensive, cute and seemingly easy to care for, but it is important to remember that, if properly nurtured, an iguana will grow rapidly, reaching maximum lengths, including the tail, of 5 feet or so. They need plenty of room, sunlight and special facilities. The larger monitor lizards also grow to relatively great lengths. They are spectacular animals and well worth the effort, but you have to be realistic about what you can provide your new lizard. There are many lizards that can be adequately housed in aquarium tanks 3 feet long and 1 foot or so wide.

Another consideration is food. Vegetarian lizards can be accommodated by the fresh or frozen produce section of your supermarket. In a pinch, monitor lizards can be fed canned dog food and the same sorts of meats, and even some vegetable matter, that we eat. A lot of lizards are insectivores. They need to be fed live insects such as crickets, wingless fruit flies, mealworms (Flour Beetle larvae) and other bugs and worms, all of which are available in your local pet or bait shop, or by mail from live food suppliers (see chapter 11, "Resources").

KEY FACTORS IN CHOOSING A LIZARD

- How much space are you willing to devote to your lizard's cage?

- If you will have more than one lizard, do you have room to house them separately, if necessary?

- Will you be willing to feed your lizard insects or rodents, or is a herbivore a better choice for you?

- Will your children and other family members be willing to learn how to properly handle a delicate lizard?

You have to decide whether to set up a live bug larder for your lizard (especially if you buy bugs via mail-order—the minimum cricket order is 1000!) or stop at the pet shop three or four times a week to buy smaller quantities of live foods. So the next questions you need to ask anyone selling you a lizard (after "how big does it get?") is "what does it eat?" and "how can I find that food conveniently and rapidly?" Unlike snakes, which can be offered a mouse once a week or every two weeks, most lizards need to eat every day or every other day.

The following section is a rough guide to the most commonly found lizards available for hobbyists. It is by no means complete, but gives a thumbnail sketch including maximum size, housing and heating needs and feeding requirements.

Texas Horned Lizard.

Horned Toads *(Phrynosoma sp.)*

More accurately called horned lizards, there are fourteen species, which range all the way from British Columbia (Canada), throughout the western third of the U.S. to Central America. Some populations are protected as endangered species. They are diurnal.

You must provide a habitat that is dry, ranging from forest to scrub to desert. Horned toads remain small, reaching a maximum of 4 to 5 inches including tail. Feeding them can be a problem because they eat mainly ants, which most pet shops do not carry. You may need to set up an ant farm to accommodate their feeding needs, although they can be encouraged to eat other small insects such as wingless fruit flies and mealworms. Horned toads release a substance into their blood that renders them immune to the toxic effects of ant venoms; they will grab and swallow live ants such as Fire Ants and Harvester Ants with impunity. Water is best given by means of a plant spray bottle. Spray the entire animal lightly around the head and it will lap up the water dripping through its scaly channels.

Although some more northern species endure a temperate climate and hibernate in colder months, activity for most species require temperatures in the 90° to 95°F range.

Savannah Monitor.

Monitor Lizards *(Varanus sp.)*

Monitors, as a group, are the largest and undoubtedly the most intelligent of the lizards. There are thirty-seven species, many of which are classified as endangered species and not available except from captive-born stocks. In addition, about two-thirds of the world's monitors, especially some of the smaller species, are found in Australia and Papua New Guinea. These are not normally available to the American hobbyist because their export is legally banned. Occasionally captive-born young or descendants of previously smuggled animals show up on the legal market in the United States.

The most commonly offered monitors are the African Nile Monitor (*Varanus niloticus*), which grows up to 7 feet; the Savannah Monitor (*Varanus exanthematicus*), measuring 3 to 5 feet at maturity and the Asian Water Monitor (*Varanus salvator*), which grows to a maximum of 8 feet! If you want calmness and docility in a monitor, then your best choice is the Savannah Monitor, which becomes very placid with frequent handling.

All monitors except Gray's Monitors are carnivores, and it is not hard to meet their nutritional requirements. In addition to insects and other invertebrates, monitors can eat hard-boiled eggs, canned dog and cat foods, fish and small rodents. Diet should be as varied as possible and vitamin and mineral supplements used, especially if you're feeding processed foods devoid of bone and organ meats, from which they normally get nutrients and minerals in the wild.

Monitors require sizable living quarters and enclosures should be at least twice as long as their ultimate or maximum size, and about half again as wide. They require temperatures in the 85° to 90°F range during the day, although some species like it slightly hotter. To help match their natural day/night cycles, temperatures at night should be allowed to drop to 70°F.

American Chameleons or Anoles (*Anolis sp.*)

There are more than 150 species of anole lizard, including six species found in the United States. Only one of these, the Carolina or Green Anole (*Anolis carolinensis;* the American Chameleon), is native. The other five species of anole are introduced species, hitchhiking here on boats, in cargo or even by air. They arrived here from Central and South America and the West Indies, usually concealed in boxes of fruit, flowers or textiles.

Anoles are the perfect "starter" lizards and are especially recommended for the novice. They are inexpensive, require minimal housing and do well in captivity if properly cared for. A single anole can live comfortably in a 5-gallon glass hooded aquarium; if more than one is going to be kept then you should allow about 5 gallons of aquarium capacity per animal. Two males will fight unless given fairly spacious surroundings to stake out their own territories. Store-bought (sterile) potting soil atop a layer of pebbles and potted or planted live vegetation can be included in their containers. Since anoles are arboreal, they should be provided with climbing branches or plants for sleeping as well as basking.

Brown Anole.

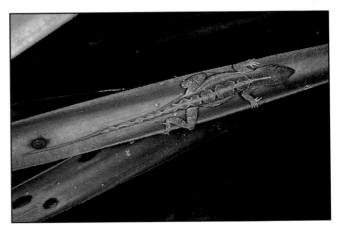

Ideal temperatures range between 70°F at night to as high as 90°F in the daytime. Anoles need at least eight hours of sunlight or full spectrum lighting daily. They eat a wide variety of small insects including small crickets, mealworms and fruit flies. Vitamin/mineral supplements can be sprinkled on the insects prior to feeding.

Fence Lizards or Swifts
(*Sceloporus sp.*)

There are close to 100 or so species and subspecies of the fence lizard or swift native to North America, and they all make interesting, easy to care for captives that adapt well if properly housed and cared for. They become so well acclimated that they'll even learn to take food from a human hand.

These lizards are small, most reaching no more than 6 inches including the tail, and several can be housed comfortably at about two to each 10 gallons of aquarium space. They like to run, so they should be given as much space as you can afford. They are animated and inquisitive. You can decorate their caging with rocks, layer it with soil or pebbles and use live plants if desired. It is important to spray the tank at least once daily with a few squirts of water, wetting the leaves and other tank structures, which these lizards will find to lap up water. A nighttime temperature of 70°F and up to 80°F in the day is sufficient for the more northern species. If you obtain a fence lizard species found in the southwest or Mexico, then somewhat warmer daytime temperatures (85° to 90°F) should be provided. They should be fed a variety of both hard and soft bodied insects including mealworms, flies, waxworms, moths and crickets. Larger animals take correspondingly larger prey.

Emerald Swift.

Even with the best of care these inexpensive lizards rarely live for more than a year and short life spans of one to two years are natural for them.

Bearded Dragons *(Pogona sp.)*

Bearded Dragons are a favorite of serious lizard fanciers. These personable and placid lizards make an excellent choice for both novices and advanced lizard hobbyists. They get their common name from their threat display. When startled or intimidated they flatten their bodies, elevate themselves on all four legs, and then erect a half-moon array of spiny scales at the rear of the lower jaw. This makes them look like they're sporting a beard!

Because all five species of Bearded Dragon are Australian, it is legally impossible to obtain wild-caught ones. However, in the mid-1980s hundreds were intercepted by authorities entering the U.S. as contraband. Since Australia didn't want them back (they're by no means an endangered species down under and are, in fact, quite common), they were given to zoos and museums and other educational or research facilities. It soon became apparent that they were not difficult to breed. In the beginning, offspring commanded prices in the hundreds of dollars. Because they are so prolific, today the wholesale price has dropped to about $30 for babies and may drop further still. Thanks to the confiscation of these smuggled lizards more than a decade ago, non-Australian hobbyists can now enjoy owning these marvelous animals. And because their price is so low and they are so easily captive-bred, it is no longer financially worthwhile for anyone to ever try illegally smuggling them out of Australia again. The case of the smuggled Bearded Dragons is one example of something good coming out of something bad, and it demonstrates that captive breeding can help fill hobbyist demand and prevent removal of animals from their wild habitat. Regrettably, not every case turns out this way.

This Bearded Dragon is displaying the neck flap for which it is named.

The most common species of Bearded Dragon available in the U.S. from captive-breeding efforts is the Central or Island species (*Pogona vitticeps*). It is a heavy bodied agamid, reaching maximum lengths of 8 to 10 inches.

The Central Beardie is omnivorous and will eat both insects and vegetation. They especially relish sweet fruits and flowers. They should be fed daily. They also eat almost any kind of small invertebrate or vertebrate, including other lizards. Hatchlings, therefore, should be kept individually and not housed with their parents or larger animals. Hatchlings will also nip on each others tails and toes, causing deformities.

Aquariums or cages can be lined with newsprint or fine (clean and sterile) sand and decorated with rock formations and branches. If you use anything other than newsprint remember they eat and defecate frequently, so their cage bottoms need to be cleaned on a daily basis. These are active lizards that need room to run and grow. Cages or aquariums should be five times longer than the lizard itself and at least 1½ to 2 feet wide so the animal has plenty of room to move around.

Under-cage heating pads should maintain a portion of the bottom of the cage at about 90°F. If they overheat they can move to an unheated part of the cage to cool off. An overhead heat light, such as a 60 to 75 watt spotlight, should be kept on twelve hours a day. Full spectrum lighting or exposure to natural, unfiltered sunlight is also important. Bearded Dragons are diurnal; they are active and feed only in light. Feed them early in the daylight part of the cycle so they have enough time to consume as much as they want before "lights out." Foods should be dusted with a vitamin/mineral supplement.

If you are feeding a diet of both vegetable matter and bugs it is advisable to feed the vegetable matter first. After most or all of it is gone, then offer insect foods. Crickets, fruit flies and mealworms are taken with relish. Feed a variety, not too much of one insect or another. The same rule applies to the salad part of the meal. Chop up yellow squash, pears, apples, carrots and their greens, dandelion greens and their flowers (if available), endive and Romaine lettuce and feed it as mixture or salad. You can try other veggies such as raw green beans, chard and sprouts to add variety. Do not offer acidic fruits such as lemon, lime or grapefruit.

A plastic refrigerator dish can be used as a pool. It should be large enough for the lizard to climb into. It will use it to both drink and soak; often it will defecate in the water, so this container should be changed and cleaned frequently, sometimes as often as once or twice a day.

True or Old-World Chameleons (*Chamaeleo sp.*)

The true or old-world chameleons, most of which originate in either Africa or on the island of Madagascar, are among the most unusual and, unfortunately, most demanding and difficult lizards to maintain and breed successfully in captivity. Chameleons are also found on Sri Lanka, in India, Pakistan, Crete, southern Spain, on the Arabian Peninsula and on some islands in the Indian Ocean. Chameleons from around the world range in size from about 1 inch to over 2 feet, although they average between 6 and 10 inches excluding the tail.

Their many quirks and special feeding and housing requirements make them a challenge to fanciers. Some hobbyists, after spending years on other easier types of lizards, may find the challenge a worthwhile and rewarding endeavor.

There are over 120 species and subspecies of true chameleons divided into four genera:

> *Bradypdion*—Dwarf Chameleons; thirteen species
>
> *Brooksia*—Leaf Chameleons; twenty-one species
>
> *Chamaeleo*—Chameleons; seventy-eight species
>
> *Rhampholeon*—Stumptail Chameleons; ten species

The biggest group, *Chamaeleo*—which means "little lion"—is most commonly available to hobbyists. Many chameleon species are scarce, difficult to obtain or are protected as endangered or threatened with extinction. The difficulty with which these lizards can be maintained and bred adds to their scarcity, and many types are best left alone within their natural habitat as their only hope of survival.

In one interesting case, the unique and startling Three-horned Jackson's Chameleon was introduced into the wild in Hawaii and is now well established on Oahu, as well as on the Kona side of the big island of Hawaii and on Maui.

*Jackson's
Chameleon.*

The subspecies in Hawaii is known as the Yellow Crested Jackson's Chameleon (*Chamaeleo jacksonii xantholopus*). All Hawaiian Jackson's Chameleons are descended from a group of a few dozen released by a pet shop owner who imported them with permission of the Hawaii State Department of Agriculture. The lizards arrived sickly, so the shop owner released them into his backyard, assuming that they could restore themselves and be retrieved later for sale. The animals not only restored themselves, they began to breed and so began to spread far and wide. Just about every one of the Yellow Crested Jackson's Chameleons (normally found in Kenya) sold in the U.S. was captured and brought here from this population introduced in Hawaii. This lizard has become a legend in Hawaii and is one of the most popular wild animals with youngsters and is widely kept as a pet there. In Hawaii they can be maintained year-round in large outdoor enclosures or compounds, and they do best this way. Duplicating this environment in a cold climate house or apartment on the mainland U.S. can be done, but is definitely a challenge. Feeding can be a problem as well, as chameleons quickly tire of the same food and must constantly be offered new types of bugs to eat. If they tire of one particular type of food they've been known to stop eating and die. Moreover, they need to gobble up large numbers of insects every day. Larger chameleons eat small birds, rodents, other lizards and small snakes as well.

They need natural, unfiltered sunlight or special UV-B emitting bulbs. Insects fed as food need to be gut loaded or dusted with vitamin/mineral supplements. Watering chameleons is also a challenge. They will not drink from a water bowl, but prefer instead to get their water from rain drops passing in front of them or lapping up dew on leaves. Various drip systems have been devised and put into use to accommodate their drinking behavior, including modification of medical IV drip sets.

Chameleons need to be housed separately or be given plenty of space as they are highly territorial and will fight with any other chameleon, male or female, that gets in their space. Males and females can be placed together to mate and breed, but should be separated after courtship and mating is completed.

They also need plenty of branches on which to perch and a cage that is higher than it is wide, preferably well aerated on three or all sides. The most commonly kept tropical species require daytime temperatures up to 90°F under a basking light. Cool and hot spots should be provided so the lizard can thermoregulate by moving back and forth. Temperatures can drop to 70°F at night. Chameleons are active and feed during daylight hours. Chameleons, as well as any plant matter used to landscape their enclosures, should be misted twice a day—in the early morning and again at dusk. A warm breeze seems to stimulate some chameleons, and some hobbyists have established elaborate warmed fan systems that cause a gentle breeze to waft through their enclosures.

And if the above special needs aren't enough, many wild-caught imports come loaded with parasites and need to be expertly and carefully diagnosed and treated by a knowledgeable veterinarian. Although some parasites are kept in check in the wild by the animal's immune system, the stresses associated with captivity may suppress immune function and then such parasites can become a real problem.

In addition to the Hawaiian Yellow Crested Jackson's Chameleon, hobbyists also have had some luck with the large Panther Chameleon (*Chamaeleo pardalis*), and either of these is recommended as a starter species for novice chameleon keepers. Regardless of which chameleon species you decide on, always opt for captive-born chameleons and buy them from a knowledgeable source that can provide continuing advice and counseling on problems that arise.

Ornate Mastigure.

Spiny-Tailed Agamids or Mastigures *(Uromastyx sp.)*

There are some fourteen species of mastigure or spiny-tailed agamids. They are almost all desert species, ranging from Saharan North Africa, into the Middle East and the arid North Indian region. They inhabit, extremely arid open sandy desert or rocky areas; they dig burrows up to 5 feet deep in order to escape harsh conditions at the surface. They obtain almost all their water from the food that they eat and reabsorb the liquid part of their urine to further conserve this precious resource. They also can be seen lapping dew or drinking rain drops that fall around their heads.

Some species are gorgeously colored in mosaics of green, red and yellow, whereas others are drab and sandy or brown colored. Among the least expensive and most commonly offered is the dark brown colored Egyptian Mastigure (*Uromastyx aegypticus*). More expensive and more rarely seen is the patterned and colorful Ornate Mastigure (*Uromastyx ornatus*). Its colors are so striking that it's hard to believe it is a real, live lizard and not an artist's conception. Another very colorful species is Dabbs Mastigure (*Uromastyx acanthinurus*), which is dotted with bands of black spots on a yellow background blending to orange-red.

Mastigures are herbivores (a few are omnivorous) and are not difficult to feed. They will consume a wide variety of store-bought vegetables, greens and fruits, which should be lightly rinsed to provide water and then dusted with a powdered vitamin/mineral supplement. In the wild, mastigures endure a diet of desert scrubs, leaves, seeds and flowers. In captivity you can feed them collard greens, kale, mustard and dandelion greens with or without flowers. Do not collect leafy matter or flowers from areas that may have been sprayed with pesticides or other agricultural chemicals.

They require a sandy or rocky habitat heated to 100° to 110°F during the day. Like other lizards they should be given a choice of cool (85°F) and hot spots (95° to 105°F) in order to thermoregulate. They will try to bury themselves in the substrate, mimicking their burrowing behavior in the wild, but unless you provide great depth they will not be able to completely submerge themselves.

They range in size from 15 inches to as long as 2½ feet (including tail) for the Egyptian Mastigure. With frequent human interaction these lizards will not struggle against handling. They almost never bite, but will try to inflict injury by whipping enemies with their powerful, spiked tails. In addition, mastigures practice tail autotomy as a defensive measure, so be careful not to intimidate them or handle them roughly lest you wind up with a less-than-perfect stub-tailed specimen.

More and more captive-born specimens are being offered; it's always a good idea to purchase these rather than wild-caught specimens because their health tends to be much better.

Mastigures require a roomy cage, with a length at least three to four times the lizard's length, a sandy substrate of 2 to 3 inches in depth (use white or color-fast sterile store-bought aquarium sand) and a number of rocks to add realism to the environment. Heat can be provided by keeping them in a warm spot in your house as well as by using a 100 watt heat bulb from above and an under-cage heating pad under a portion of the enclosure. Mastigures definitely like it hot and won't eat or be active if temperatures drop too low which, in their case, is 85°F or less. Temperatures up to 120° F are easily tolerated by most species of this group since they come from some of the most torrid deserts in the world.

Natural, unfiltered sunlight is a plus, but if it's not available, use a fluorescent tube capable of emitting UV-B light. If the sides of your enclosure are high enough, it is not necessary to cover or lid the top as these lizards are not great climbers or jumpers. This gives you the opportunity of opening a window during warm days and allowing the enclosure to be bathed in sunlight unfiltered by a glass or screen top.

Chinese Water Dragons
(*Physignathus cocincinus sp.*)

The Chinese or Oriental Water Dragon is found in southeast Asia and parts of southern China. Growing to lengths of 3 feet, these iguana look-alikes (they are not iguanids but actually agamids) are lively and growing in popularity. They live in trees and bushes and frequently enter ground water to cool off and/or escape predators. This lizard is capable of changing shades, becoming light green at higher temperatures (85°F or above) and darker tans and browns at lower temperatures.

Chinese Water Dragon (juvenile).

They require roomy cages at least 4 feet long, 2 feet wide and 3 feet high, densely planted with foliage and branches for them to climb. Substrate can range from sterile store-bought loam or sandy soils (with plants that do well in these kinds of soils or kept in pots external to the substrata). A large pool of water, occupying as much as one-third of the ground area, should be provided. A small airpump powering an airstone should be placed in the water to increase ambient humidity and prevent stagnation. Like other lizards, Chinese Water Dragons are apt to foul their water with waste products, so the water should be cleaned and changed daily.

These lizards are omnivorous and readily accept both insects and vegetarian foods. They eat crickets, mealworms, waxworms, earthworms, guppies and goldfish (which can be placed in their pool) as well as fruit flies, moths and other bugs. On the vegetarian side, they should be offered squash, cooked corn niblets (no butter please), shredded carrots plus a variety of greens including dandelion, collards and mustard greens.

They are diurnal, and daytime temperatures should be maintained in the mid-80s, and not be allowed to drop below 75°F at night. They need warm and cool spots and a basking light from above in addition to a UV-B source.

Basilisk Lizards *(Basilicus sp.)*

There are several species of *Basilicus* seen in the pet trade but the Green Basilisk (*Basilicus plumifrons*) is one of the most popular. The Brown or Striped Basilisk (*Basilicus vittatus*) and the Common Basilisk (*Basilicus basicilicus*) are also available. These are relatively large, nervous animals that reach lengths of 3 feet including the tail. Their head and dorsal crests give them an eerie prehistoric appearance that undoubtedly contributes to their popularity. They are territorial and keeping more than one male at a time in confined quarters can lead to squabbling.

Plumed Basilisk (juvenile).

They should be given plenty of room as they like to race. In the wild these are the lizards best known for the ability to run across the water, thanks to specialized scales on the bottoms of their rear feet. Because of their edgy demeanor they do not make good handling lizards. And if one happens to get away from you its great speed would make it difficult to recapture unless cornered. As display animals, however, they are second to none. It's best to keep no more than a single male, perhaps with one or two females, in a large enclosure measuring at least 4 feet by 2 feet and $2\frac{1}{2}$ to 3 feet high. They like to climb, so the cage should be furnished with plenty of branches and either artificial or live foliage. Temperatures in the mid-80s during the day, not dropping below 72°F at night, should be maintained. Although 60 to 70 percent relative humidity is adequate, these lizards are more apt to mate and breed if the humidity levels are raised to 85 to 90 percent. This can be done with a glass cover, a large pool of water and an airstone to circulate the moisture. Misting the tank several times a day also helps raise humidity levels, as do live plants, which help to retain moisture.

Basilisks can be fed a wide variety of insects including crickets, mealworms, *Zoophobia* or giant mealworms, waxworms, spiders, moths and flies. They can also eat newborn mice but should not be fed these more than once a week.

They can be fed daily or every other day. At least once every four days it is a good idea to dust food with a vitamin/mineral supplement or gut load their prey items with such preparations.

Legless Lizards—Various types

There are only a few legless lizards found in the United States; the Baja California Legless Lizard (*Anniella geronimensis*), and the California Legless Lizard (*Anniella pulchra*), are examples. These lizards are members of the *Anguidae* or lateral fold lizard group.

These lizards make unpopular terrarium inhabitants because they're almost entirely fossorial—not only burrowing beneath the substrata but remaining and even feeding there as well. They are easy to keep and can be kept housed in a 10-gallon tank lined with fine, loosely packed store-bought sand. They need to be sprayed lightly about once a week and readily accept a diet of mealworms, waxworms, slugs, ants and small crickets. They need to be fed only once a week. Once the insects are placed in the container and burrow into the sand, the lizards will find them. The lizards need to be kept cool, not higher than 70° to 75°F, so no special heating or lighting arrangements are usually necessary.

As fascinating and as easy to care for as these lizards are, they don't attract many adherents because of their secretive habits. Because native California wildlife cannot be collected without a permit, California Legless Lizards are not readily available. However, other legless lizards such as the Glass "Snakes" are occasionally available; they are very similar to the California Legless Lizards.

*Blue-tongued
Skink.*

Blue-Tongued Skinks
(Tiliqua sp.)

There are over 1,000 species of skinks, so it is virtually impossible to give care and keeping advice about all of them. One of the most popular species is the Blue-tongued Skink of the genus *Tiliqua,* of which there are some eleven fairly similar species. The majority of these (all, in fact, save one) are found in Australia. The Giant Blue-tongued Skink (*Tiliqua gigas*), is found from Papua New Guinea north to Indonesia and westward to Sumatra. Because of the ban on export of

Australian animals it is this species that is most frequently offered in the U.S. The offspring of confiscated smuggled or legally obtained zoo/research Australian species are occasionally available as well. If you are considering some other kind of skink, it is necessary to research their dietary, temperature and housing requirements.

Blue-tongued Skinks are among the largest members of the skink family, reaching lengths of nearly 2 feet and living up to twenty years. They are territorial, so are best housed separately except when breeding. Their most striking feature is their bright blue tongue, which they flash at would-be attackers as a warning. Most of the time it startles and scares off predators.

They are diurnal ground dwellers and need to be given both hot and cool spots in their enclosures in order to thermoregulate. Because they obtain heat from the ground, an under-cage heating mat under a portion of the enclosure is the best way to provide this warmth. Temperatures between 85° and 90° F are optimal.

They need sizable enclosures, at least three to four times as long as the lizard itself and about 2 feet wide. A length of large bore (4 to 6 inches) PVC pipe should be provided as a hidebox. Substrate can be artificial turf carpeting, plain newsprint or paper toweling. Artificial plants as well as decorative rocks can be placed to landscape the quarters. They are pretty easy to feed. While primarily carnivorous, diced up fruits and vegetables can be added to a meat- or chow-based diet. In addition to crickets, mealworms, *Zoophobias*, giant mealworms and newborn mice, they'll eat moistened dog chow as well as canned dog and cat food. These lizards eat so well and so voraciously they become obese in no time, so it may be necessary to put your lizard on a diet to keep its weight down. They will drink from a water bowl and should have fresh water available at all times.

Like other lizards they are prone to metabolic bone disease; in this species MBD frequently manifests itself as a condition called "rubber jaw" and spinal curvature. It

is prevented by appropriate vitamin/mineral supple-
mentation and UV-B lighting.

Eyelid or Leopard Geckos (*Eublepharis sp.*)

As their common name implies, these lizards have
spots and true movable eyelids. Unlike other geckos,
they lack the adhesive pads geckos use for wall climbing; instead their toes terminate in tiny claws. All members of this group occur either in the United States or
in northern India, Pakistan and Afghanistan. They survive in dry regions, and *Eublepharis macularius* reaches
lengths of up to 8 to 10 inches, which makes it a relatively large member of the gecko group of lizards.
Their close relatives, the banded geckos (*Coleonyx sp.*),
are also eyelid geckos and available to hobbyists. Care
for these is similar to care for the Leopard Geckos.

*Leopard Gecko
(Eublepharis
macularius).*

These lizards can be comfortably housed singly or in
pairs in 10 to 20-gallon aquariums with store-bought
(sterilized) sand as substrate. The aquarium can be further decorated with cacti or other desert succulents.
Flat rocks or pieces of shale go nicely with this decor
and can be used to dress up the display. These lizards
sleep under shelter, and so it is necessary to construct
tiny caves or create crevices between and under rocks
for this purpose. Pet shops also carry rocklike artificial

75

hides suitable for small lizards to curl up inside. Ideally these lizards should be housed singly; two or more males should never be kept together.

Geckos are insectivores and should be offered feeder bugs such as crickets, mealworms, fruit flies and moths of a size that they can subdue and swallow easily. They will lap up water on spray-misted plants and from puddles created on rock formations, and can be encouraged to drink from a small, shallow water bowl.

Geckos are primarily nocturnal but will be abroad in daylight as well, especially if food is present. Because they obtain heat primarily from the ground, part of their tank should have an under-cage heating pad. Temperatures in the mid-80s are optimal.

Iguanas *(Iguana sp.)*

The common Green Iguana (*Iguana iguana*) is probably the most widely kept reptile of any kind. Part of the reason for its seemingly endless popularity is its low price, easy availability and small size—just 8 to 10 inches including the tail. As an adult it is truly a spectacular animal.

Green Iguana.

Cared for properly, Green Iguanas can reach lengths of 5 feet and weights of 15 pounds or so. They need plenty of room as they grow; many iguana lovers have turned entire rooms in their homes into iguana dens.

Iguanas are strict vegetarians and should be fed a nutritious and highly varied diet of leafy greens, fruits and vegetables. They will eat pasta and bread and other human foods, but these should be avoided in favor of the iguana-salad approach. Foods may also be lightly dusted with a vitamin/mineral supplement. There is an extensive body of literature on iguana diet and nutrition as well as the problems that befall these lizards if improperly fed. Among the items recommended for iguanas are collard greens, dandelion greens with or without flowers, shredded carrots, kale, kohlrabi, sliced yellow squash and bits of apple, orange, berries and grapes (but not too many). Iguanas also love any kind of lettuce, but lettuce is of no value nutritionally to them so it should be avoided. If they get used to eating lettuce they will forgo other foods and this is not a good thing.

THE TERRITORIAL IGUANA

If you are considering getting an iguana, you are best off keeping only one. Iguanas are quite territorial, and fights between iguanas do occur. In fact, iguanas that have lived together for a long time may suddenly attack one another, seemingly out of nowhere. An iguana may even challenge its owner in a fit of territorialism.

In addition, they need eight to twelve hours a day of UV-B exposure, either from a special fluorescent light or from unfiltered sunlight, an impossibility during the winter months in more temperate as well as northern climates.

They obtain water from their food, which can be wetted prior to feeding and, in addition, they lap up spray-mist as well as drink from a water bowl. They also like to swim; as they get larger they are best accommodated in the family bathtub after all traces of soap or cleaning agents have been rinsed away. In addition, it is necessary to disinfect the tub afterwards because iguanas, like all reptiles, shed salmonella bacteria, which is potentially pathogenic to humans. If you set aside a separate room it may not be a bad idea to include a shallow kiddie pool for this purpose. Filling and emptying it will challenge the iguana owner's ingenuity. Be careful not to let splashes reach your eyes or mouth, or come in contact with any open cuts.

If you are bent on getting an iguana or already have one, it's a good idea to read the abundance of literature on them. They are easily calmed when handled frequently (at least most of them) and make otherwise excellent and spectacular pets.

Tegu Lizards *(Tupinambis sp.)*

The common tegu lizard is a heavy bodied, strikingly marked Black and White South American Lizard (*Tupinambis teguixin*), which reaches lengths up to 2½ feet, approximately half of which is tail. Although there are more than 200 different species of tegu lizard, the most commonly available in addition to the common tegu are a Gold and Black, and Red and Black form, which aside from color, are just about identical.

*Red Tegu
(juvenile).*

Tegus eat a variety of foods and are not difficult to feed or supplement with vitamins and minerals. In addition to small mice and *Zoophobia* larvae, tegus will eat dog food, hard-boiled eggs, lean cooked meats and animal chows. They become overweight rather easily, so they should not be overfed.

Because of their size they need spacious quarters and are best housed alone as they can be territorial. Even if raised from juveniles, they do not tame easily and have irritable dispositions. Large adults can inflict a nasty bite, so such animals should be handled with care, if at all. Their sharp claws are also formidable weapons and can inflict deep, painful welts. Although they climb in low-lying brush they are principally ground-dwelling lizards and branches and perches are not necessary.

Tegus are diurnal, and temperatures at 85° to 90°F during daytime and 70° to 75°F at night are preferred.

Caring
for
Your

part three

Lizard

chapter 7

Housing
Your
Lizard

A variety of pre-built commercial enclosures, including aquarium tanks, Iguanariums™, pre-built cages and other structures, can be used to house your lizard. The nature and size of the enclosure depends mainly on the nature and size of the lizard you have. Smaller lizards, ranging from a few inches to 2 feet in size, can be housed in pre-built all-glass aquariums of the appropriate size, fitted with screen covers and lighting fixtures. Some small burrowing lizards can be comfortably kept in sand-filled gallon jars with a minimum of other considerations. However, proper accommodation for most lizards involves more than four walls and a cover. The lizard keeper must also provide proper lighting, heating, substrate or flooring, plants, decorations and other cage furnishings, such as water bowls and hideboxes.

Caging

When setting up your lizard's home it is better to err on the side of too much space rather than too little. The vast majority of first-time lizard owners, particularly those who opt for lizards that reach considerable size, often place their new lizards in structures that are far too small for their needs. Size guidelines are given in chapter 6. They range from a gallon jug sufficient for a small burrowing legless lizard to structures 10 feet long, 7 feet high and 2½ feet wide for large arboreal species such as the common Green Iguana. If you build your own enclosure or have one custom built, make sure it will be big enough for your lizard's future

needs. Be sure to design your lizard's home for easy cleaning and maintenance. Enclosures for climbing or arboreal species should include shelves and the means to attach branches to the upper reaches of their walls. The flooring should be easy to clean. Vinyl-tile flooring or

This juvenile Spiny-tailed Iguana is quickly outgrowing its enclosure.

glass-bottomed structures such as large aquarium tanks are examples. Substrate should be selected with the lizard's needs and your planting and decorating objectives in mind. If an aquarium is used, the top should not be glass-covered except for species that require high humidity. Screen covers are best. If a cage is being built, grate-covered ventilation holes can be made in the sides and back wall. Some hobbyists prefer hinged doors, others sliding doors. Aquariums covered with screen covers mean performing chores through the top. A number of companies that advertise in reptile magazines advertise standard and custom cage building services. These cages are made from nontoxic materials laminated with melamine or Formica™. Be sure any glues, paints or other substances applied to the tank are not toxic after properly dried.

SIZE

I keep a 4-foot iguana comfortably in a 4 foot long, 1½ foot wide cage. It is 6 feet high, and it's height that this guy is looking for. The zoo does likewise, and so do most knowledgeable hobbyists. The cage should be as long, as wide and as high as is necessary for the lizard to comfortably turn around. Arboreal or perching species such as iguanas and chameleons prefer height, whereas ground dwellers benefit from greater surface area.

For this reason, a good option for large and arboreal lizards is flight cages or aviaries. These can be custom built or ordered pre-fabricated or knock-down from your local pet shop. They can be installed indoors (with enough space) and moved out-of-doors when the weather becomes hotter. They allow sunlight, unfiltered by glass, to warm your iguanas or other large lizards, and because of their height they can be outfitted with branches, perches or vines for your lizard to climb. Obviously they are not suitable for lizards small enough to escape between the caging bars, and they are not suitable for lizards that need a high humidity environment. They are also more difficult to heat properly than an enclosed cage, but this is not impossible.

NO CAGE AT ALL?

Some folks don't mind if their lizards are allowed to "free roam." This certainly solves the cage size problem and lets you provide special requirements by rearranging a room to share with your lizard. Some people design their whole apartment or home around a group of free roaming iguanas. There are, however, a few important considerations before you go this route.

It is important to remember that all reptiles, including lizards, may have salmonella bacteria on their bodies and may shed it in their feces and deposit it on surfaces merely by walking there. Therefore, free roaming lizards should be prohibited from traveling in areas or on surfaces where food is prepared or served. They should also be kept out of the bathroom, since toothbrushes and other personal hygiene articles could become contaminated. If you provide a perch near a window (be sure it is closed in winter and screened in summer), lizards such as iguanas will spend a good deal of their time basking and watching from such vantage points well off the ground. They may descend to defecate and to eat or lay eggs. Allowing your lizards free run of one or two rooms in your house also means giving them warm spots with human heating pads and basking lights or heating elements. Alternatively you need climate control, and you must keep the room warm enough for their needs. This is too warm for most people. Humans prefer temperatures ranging from the mid-60s to mid-70s and feel uncomfortable at higher temperatures for prolonged periods. So unless you like it as hot as your lizards, this isn't a workable alternative. Some lizard fanciers keep their animals in or near furnace rooms. If you do this, make sure the venting system is working properly, as any excess carbon monoxide from gas or oil burners can asphyxiate your lizard. Don't use your lizard as the reptile equivalent of a miner's canary. Have your heating system professionally serviced and checked regularly. Since the thermostat for a furnace is apt to be somewhere else in the house, such rooms frequently overheat or remain too cool, so you should check the temperatures over time if you decide on this option.

Finally, hazards must be removed. Large free roaming iguanas can shred and pull down curtains, knock over lamps and other household items and get tripped up in electrical wires. Whatever room you decide to let your large lizards roam in must be lizard-proofed.

THOUGHTS ON AQUARIUMS

Although aquariums add beauty to your home, they may not be the best housing choice for your lizard. The glass of aquariums can block the beneficial rays of the sun and also intensify the heat. They can also be difficult to clean, especially if moisture accumulates in the substrate. This in turn may result in an unsanitary, and unpleasant living condition for your lizard. Never keep a true chameleon in an aquarium. When these lizards see their reflection in the aquarium glass, they think that they are seeing another chameleon, causing them great stress.

Lighting

Lighting is especially important for lizards. All lizards except burrowing species need two types of lighting fixtures. They require a suitably sized fluorescent fixture in which UV-A and UV-B bulbs can be used. Incandescent light fixtures are also required for ceramic heating elements or incandescent bulbs, either of which will produce much-needed aerial heat. Non–light producing heating elements, as well as certain high wattage bulbs, require a ceramic insulated socket for safety purposes.

Cages can be beautiful additions to a living room, but they must provide the lizard essentials of heat, protection and warmth.

A fluorescent fixture is unnecessary if you have an alternative way to provide eight to twelve hours a day of unfiltered natural sunlight. Access to this amount of sunlight is often an impossibility, especially in colder climates, so fluorescent fixtures and special bulbs are often the only choice. Some lizard fanciers have constructed cages within window boxes made from UV light admitting glass. Normal plate glass panes filter out UV light. UV light admitting glass is expensive, but can make a special lighting fixture unnecessary. It is available at hardware stores, or can be special ordered through most window companies and contractors. Because it is such an expensive investment, most novice lizard fanciers opt for the more portable and initially less expensive lighting alternative.

Without the right amount of UV-B lighting, lizards are unable to manufacture vitamin D3. Vitamin D3 deficiency causes bone loss and a condition known as metabolic bone disease, or MBD. It is more prevalent and serious in growing lizards than in fully grown adults, but can cause problems at any age. Lizards need a combination of proper diet and lighting in order to prevent MBD. MBD ultimately results in weakened bones—especially of the limbs, jaw and vertebral column. Eventually, a lizard with MBD will die prematurely of complications associated with this condition.

PREPACKAGED LIGHTING

Several manufacturers package UV light emitting bulbs for the pet trade. Such lights are rated by a procedure known as spectrophotometry, which measures amounts of colored light emission. Manufacturers of these bulbs can provide certified copies of spectrophotometric analyses for their products. In addition, some companies now manufacture room sized UV light emitting panels, aimed at people with circadian rhythm and seasonal affective disorder (SAD). These panels can provide a room full of UV light for entire lizard collections and larger lizards that are given free roaming privileges.

Ideally, for most lizards you should use the higher output lamps and keep them running about twelve hours a day. The light source should be placed about 15 to 18 inches from the animal's most convenient or usual basking spot. The lower output lamps would have to be on twenty-four hours a day in

> ### HOW CLOSE TO THE LIGHT?
>
> Regardless of the type of bulb you choose, the standard safe distances should apply:
>
> - A 75-watt bulb should be 1½ feet away from basking area.
> - A 100-watt bulb should be 2 feet away.
> - A 150-watt bulb should be at least 2½ to 3 feet away, depending on household temperatures.

order to provide the same amount of UV as the higher output lamps, and be kept on more than twenty-seven hours at a stretch to mimic the amount of UV light an animal gets in nature at the equator. In any case, any amount of UV-B is better than none, and in captivity with proper diet, even a small amount given twelve hours a day helps to prevent MBD and its complications. It is also important not to overdose your lizard on such light. Prolonged day cycles and light that is too intense for prolonged periods may stress your animals. A hidebox or shade helps lizards to escape from inappropriate lighting, but this solution is not always an option for larger species such as iguanas and monitors.

Spectroline radiometers are used to measure UV-A and UV-B light and can be ordered from your local pet shop. These devices may also be helpful in determining the amount of UV emitted by a bulb before and after it is filtered through glass, Plexiglas, screening or Mylar. In addition, UV emitting bulbs tend to wear down with time and their output decreases. A handheld radiometer can help the serious hobbyist to check on the extent of such degradation and alert him or her when it's time to change bulbs.

This Green Iguana is enjoying an elaborate enclosure with a beautiful background scene, branches for climbing and decorative artificial plants.

Plants

There are pros and cons to the use of live plants in lizard housing. Among the benefits are their decorative appeal and assist with climate control; plants give an enclosure a natural appearance and help maintain humidity, which is required by many tropical rain forest species. They also offer lizards that like to climb or hide an opportunity to do so. On the negative side is their maintenance and the risk that a plant you choose for its appearance may be toxic to your animals, especially herbivores who might take a munch or two from its leaves. You should be especially careful about selecting live house or garden plants if you allow larger lizards to free roam or keep them in outdoor enclosures during the hot weather.

Lizards can be poisoned by plants not only by eating them as herbivores and omnivores are apt to do, but also, in some cases, from casual contact. In addition, nursery plants, even if they are not dangerous themselves, may be sprayed with chemicals or fertilized with substances that may be toxic to lizards not only through eating (herbivorous species), but also through mere contact or tongue-flicking (all species). The Internet Web site listed in chapter 11 can point you to lists of plants toxic to iguanas and other lizards.

Live plants require soil, and the presence of soil in a lizard enclosure also offers crickets, mealworms and other bugs being fed to your animals a convenient place to hide, making feeding more difficult. Larger lizards and lizards that like to dig are apt to uproot plants as well. Therefore, considerable thought and planning must go into any decision to use live plants. Artificial plants dispel some of these concerns, but provide surface areas for bacteria and molds to grow, so they must be removed and cleaned routinely.

Many hobbyists opt for a more sterile environment. It is easier to maintain but not as pleasing to look at. The decision should be based on how much work you want to put into maintaining a lizard habitat weighed against your desire for a decorative setup.

Heating

Proper heating is nearly important to a lizard as lighting and feeding. As ectotherms, all lizards must be maintained at temperature levels that sustain activities including digestion and metabolism of food and absorption of critical nutrients. Achieving such levels is not always as easy as it seems; the ins and outs of lizard heating should be high on the lizard lover's "must learn" list.

Heating can be accomplished by three different methods, a combination of two or the third method alone. The first method is a device known as a "hot rock." It is basically a heating element that has been encased in a ceramic replica of a stone or rock. Variations include ceramic caves, hideboxes and branches wired with internal heaters. The principle behind these devices is to mimic a reptile's natural tendency to seek out belly warmth or heat by laying on rocks, paved roads or branches that retain the heat of the sun. The problem with many of these devices is their reputation to malfunction, overheat and burn the reptile in the process. The makers of these devices offer little in the way of a guarantee and provide no data about the amount of heat produced. These devices are extremely simple and have no safety cutoffs or thermostats to prevent overheating. Lizards in the process of thermoregulating, or obtaining heat to aid in digestion, will not move off a hot rock even if it starts to burn them. If the device should overheat and malfunction, the results can be disastrous for the animal. In addition, these devices heat unevenly and develop hot spots that also cause thermal injury to lizards. It is therefore recommended that hot rocks and other cage furniture, such as caves or branches wired to produce heat, be avoided or used very carefully and monitored frequently. Some suggest that hot rocks be wrapped in toweling to buffer the animal from hot spots. This obviates their function as a decorative item, so there is really little point in trying to make them safer by doing this. And a towel wrapped around a malfunctioning heater may be a fire hazard.

A safer alternative for the provision of belly heat is an under-cage or under-tank heating pad. These devices are separated from direct contact with the animal by the bottom of the cage and a layer of substrate or cage flooring material such as artificial grass, sand or even newspapers or towels. The temperature of under-cage heating pads can be monitored and hooked to a thermostat that will shut the device off when a pre-selected temperature is reached. Temperature is monitored by inserting a probe into the substrate or placing it in the space between the heating pad and the cage bottom.

Iguanas and many other kinds of lizards are heliotherms—they bask in the sun in order to thermoregulate. Getting their heat from the sun serves them in two ways: They get to warm up and obtain much needed UV-B light for vitamin D3 synthesis and healthy bones. So while direct warmth on the ventral or belly side of the lizard aids in the digestive process, basking in sunlight helps in other ways.

THE RIGHT AMOUNT OF HEAT

How much heat is enough? With a few notable exceptions, temperatures exceeding 95°F are too high for most tropical, neotropical and temperate zone lizards. The amount of heat that should be used depends on where a particular species is from. Thus certain desert lizards from particularly hot zones operate efficiently at 100° to 105°F. Iguanas, for the most part, need temperatures between 85° and 95°F during active hours, or about twelve hours a day, and nighttime temperatures should drop to between 75° and 80°F. As a rule of thumb, almost any lizard can endure nighttime drops of about 10° less than daytime temperature. If you need to use an incandescent lighting fixture to maintain nighttime temperatures, a dark colored (e.g. red or blue) bulb should be used. Heat from above can also be provided by screw-in ceramic heat emitting elements that give no light whatsoever. These must be used in ceramic sockets and be well protected against contact with anything that might burn at higher temperatures, such as plastic, wood or the lizard itself. They are best rigged or mounted between 18 and 24 inches away from the screen cover of your enclosure. Your reptile supply store may have or be able to order deep blue incandescent bulbs, which provide heat from above while emitting little or no light.

If you are on the forgetful side or are away from home occasionally, you can use timers to operate your lighting fixtures. It is also possible, by using a dimmer switch and thermostat, to turn lights up and down gradually in relation to the temperature measured.

BE CAREFUL NOT TO OVERHEAT

If lizards are overheated they may not necessarily cook, but they can stop feeding, become stressed and die of cardiac arrest. So while its important to provide heat, it is also important to remember that too much is as bad as too little. One way to help combat this problem is to make sure your lizards are housed in larger than needed enclosures and that a portion of their enclosure remains either unheated or 10° cooler than the heated part. This is easily accomplished by strategically placing your under-cage heating pad under only one side of the cage or tank, your incandescent basking or ceramic heat emitting element just abutting it and having nothing over the remaining one-third of the cage area. This sets up three zones of varying temperatures and enables your lizard to thermoregulate at will. If you are housing arboreal lizards or lizards that like to bask while perched on a branch, then you must also try to provide a top to bottom thermal gradient as well as a side to side and back to front gradient. The best way to do this is by experimenting with various light and heating pad placements using strategically placed thermometers. Pet shops sell high reading (to 105°F) reptile thermometers. If you use household thermometers that top off at lower temperatures they are apt to explode at the tips. And if you don't want to be constantly moving the thermometer to check temperatures at different spots, then it is a good idea to invest in two or three thermometers. This enables simultaneous readings from different spots in the cage. These pet shop thermometers are not the most accurate devices, and it is important to remember that a few degrees difference, especially at the high end (105°F), can mean your lizard is being exposed to excessive temperatures. A good mercury thermometer that reads accurately at high levels can be used to calibrate or check other temperature measuring devices. Locating such thermometers can be as easy as asking your local high school or college chemistry or biology department for a nearby or mail-order source. Don't leave such a thermometer in the tank unsupervised, or permanently, as your lizard is apt to knock it down and break it.

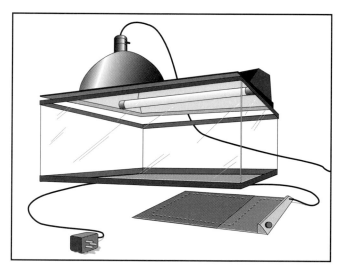

Provide your lizard with an overhead as well as an under-tank heater, but make sure you establish cooler and warmer parts of the tank so your pet can thermoregulate.

Finally, it is important to remember that just one type of heat is not sufficient for most types of lizards and that both under-cage heating pads and heat sources from above are necessary to accomplish adequate heating. By using a combination of methods you are able to warm up the air temperature as well as the substrata, and this is the best way of assuring proper activity levels, digestion and metabolism of food.

Ponds and Waterfalls

Although there are no lizards that are fully aquatic, many like to enter the water from time to time to cool off or to help them shed their skin and of course, many species come to the water's edge to drink. Large semi-aquatic species like Water Monitors and the Chinese Water Dragons benefit not only from spacious quarters, but from a large tub of water as well. Small to medium sized kitty litter pans or oversized plastic refrigerator storage bowls and dishes can easily be converted for such use. They are easy to clean and waterproof. It has been suggested by some iguana hobbyists that placing your large iguana in a bathtub or kiddy pool full of warm water and allowing it to swim around for awhile is not only healthy exercise, but helps the animal eliminate waste products in the process. Whether all iguanas need such service to remain regular is debatable, but the tactic does help relieve constipation.

A variety of smaller decorative stoneware ponds and waterfall setups are available in pet shops. These are quite attractive as well as useful, and make a worthwhile addition to a decorative lizard cage or aquarium. A plain lizard cage need only contain a small water dish. Such "ponds" can range from shallow (¼ to ½ inch lip) ashtrays to dog or cat feeding bowls. Pet shops sell these in heavyweight glazed ceramic that are difficult for any lizard to push over and spill. These bowls are easy to clean but must be discarded and replaced when the glaze wears off the inside of the bowl.

This housing setup includes logs as hiding places, easily cleaned newspaper substrate, desert plants and a tasty snack of clover! (African Mastigure)

A small airpump with tubing and airstone attached, inserted into a water dish or pond, helps break the water's surface tension, keeps it moving and adds considerably to the relative humidity of the enclosure. The bubbles of water may also help stimulate some species to breed and others to drink.

Backgrounds

Originally designed for all-glass aquariums, background landscapes are also available in a variety of reptile habitats. These scenes can be affixed to the back of an all-glass aquarium and make your lizard look as if its living in the rain forest, jungle, desert or rocky scrub-lands. One company has developed a foam rubber background that has built-in caves and can be inserted in the back of a cage or aquarium. Heavyweight shale-stone backgrounds, available for the tropical fish tank, can be diverted for use in some kinds of lizard setups. These are quite heavy, and if not properly anchored to stand in the back of the cage or aquarium they can fall and crush your lizard.

Electric Power Sources

Your lizard setup is apt to contain three or more sep-arate electrical appliances including heating pads, at least two different kinds of lighting fixtures and electronically operated thermostats. Perhaps you will even have an airpump to aerate your lizard's pond. Accordingly, thought must be given to providing safe, adequate grounded electrical sources so that these devices can all operate simultaneously without blowing a fuse or tripping a circuit breaker. Even though one or two of these devices can be plugged into a three way on a single electrical outlet, plugging everything in a mish-mash of wires into the same outlet is a bad idea. Try to find the highest amperage outlet available and attach a fused power strip and surge protector to it, into which these separate devices can then be plugged. A timer can be used to work the lighting and a ther-mostat, and a separate outlet can be used to work the under-cage heating pads. If you're away from home overnight on a cold night and a fuse blows, some species of lizards could die from the sudden tempera-ture drop if you are relying on the heating pads or lamps to provide them with warmth while the rest of the home remains cool.

chapter 8

Feeding
Your Lizard

Bearded Dragon

All lizards fall within one of three categories when it comes to diet: carnivorous (meat eaters), herbivorous (vegetarians) and omnivorous (meat and vegetable eaters). Scientists further divide animals into separate categories based on the principal dietary items. Thus, most carnivorous lizards are insectivores or insect eaters; some, of course, will eat other invertebrates and vertebrates and in captivity a few will even eat dog food! Most herbivorous lizards will eat a variety of vegetable matter. Out of the thousands of different lizard species relatively few are omnivorous.

Feeding Insectivorous Lizards

The nutritional value of insect prey and other carnivorous food matter varies considerably. Lizards are like people—they thrive on and prefer a varied diet. True chameleons, in fact, are known to stop eating and starve themselves to death when offered one type of insect continuously. Chameleons offered a varied diet never develop this sort of eating disorder.

Any pet shop that sells live reptiles also sells live insect foods. There are three good reasons for this: they need the bugs to feed their own animals, they are obligated to sell food and supplies for the animals they sell and thirdly, by so doing, they get you to come back often! You can also breed and raise your own insects but a lot of people don't want to be bothered with this. Whatever you do, don't go out and collect insects from the wild (or your basement) to feed to your lizards. Not only can they be carry all kinds of bacteria on their bodies, they could also carry pesticides or other toxic residues that can poison your lizard.

CRICKETS

You can buy crickets at your local pet shop for 10 cents each or less. You can also buy box loads of 1,000, separated by sizes (from extremely tiny to full grown and everything in between) for $10 to $15 plus overnight or two-day (in warmer weather) postage charges. The postage costs as much as or slightly more than the crickets themselves, so it doesn't pay to buy less than a 1,000 by mail order. If you buy this many you need to set up a cricket tank. A 20-gallon or larger tank with a fine mesh screen cover works and can accommodate a thousand small ("pinhead") to medium sized crickets with no problem. It should be littered with toilet paper or paper towel cardboard tubes. The crickets crawl inside these tubes and all you need to do to feed some to your lizard is to remove a tube and shake it into your lizard's enclosure until the desired number of crickets fall out. A listing of live cricket dealers is included in the resource directory.

Crickets can be dusted with vitamin/mineral powders specially formulated for reptiles and in addition can be "gut loaded" to provide extra nutritional value for your lizard. Crickets are normally fed chunks of raw white potato. Instead, you can add sections of oranges, apples and other fruits and vegetables to their diet. This in turn is delivered to your cricket-eating lizard without it ever realizing you are making it eat fruit and vegetables!

Crickets are a nutritious meal for your insectivorous lizard. (Panther Chameleon)

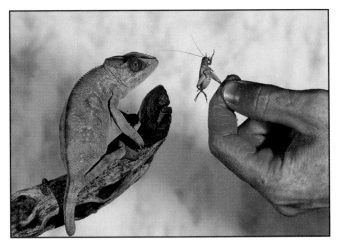

FRUIT FLIES (*DROSOPHILA MELANOGASTER* AND OTHER SPECIES)

Wingless fruit flies and specially bred flightless fruit flies are excellent insect food for small lizards. Pet shops don't carry them but mail-order dealers sell starter cultures. They are easy to raise yourself and take up very little space. A culture of these flies consists of a special fruit fly medium (food) in a pint sized glass milk jar covered with a piece of cloth held in place by a rubber band. You can buy starter cultures, extra media and complete instructions from the resources listed in the back of this book.

WAXWORMS (*GALLERIA MELONELLA* LARVAE)

Waxworms are available in pet shops, bait shops and from biological supply houses. They are the larval form of the Greater Waxmoth. These insects get their name from their propensity to destroy bee hives by eating their wax; don't let these larvae or the adult moth escape because they could destroy commercial and natural beehives in your area. They are a great lizard food and are highly nutritious. Newly formed larvae don't change to adult moths for about forty days, so quantities can be stocked without fear of them changing before they're used. While they're easily cultured, they are so inexpensive most people prefer to buy them.

MEALWORMS (*TENEBRIO MOLITOR*)

Mealworms are the wormlike larvae of the Flour Beetle. They are a popular and convenient food for insect-eating lizards and are available from most pet shops.

No lizard should be fed a steady diet of these larvae because, although high in protein, they have little calcium. They can, however, be dusted with a vitamin/mineral powder prior to feeding. A variant of these larvae are Giant Mealworms, which are simply large *Tenebrio* larvae and *Zoophobia*, a different species that is really large and makes excellent fodder for larger insectivorous lizards. Mealworms can be gut loaded by mixing powdered calcium carbonate or bone meal with bran flakes. Pieces of orange or apple can provide moisture, but be sure they are discarded promptly if a greenish-blue fungus starts to form on them. Many fungi are quite toxic and will kill your mealworms as well as poison your lizards should traces be present on the exterior of any mealworm eaten by them.

Mealworms are easy to store if other household members don't mind a covered container of these in the fridge. Their "meal" is oatmeal flakes and flour. They change into beetles in four to six months, but without notice, so buy just enough to feed your lizard(s) for a few weeks or so. The hard-shelled beetles may be eaten by some species but are largely inedible and can cause intestinal blockage if too many are ingested at once. The same may be true of the larvae since unmolted mealworms have a chitinous outer coat that is indigestible as well. Unmolted mealworms are golden colored; freshly molted, soft-bodied mealworms are creamy white. Whenever possible try to offer them to your lizard while in their soft-bodied state.

Your lizard will enjoy a variety of worms, easily available from pet shops and through the mail. (Bearded Dragon)

EARTHWORMS (*LUMBRICUS SP.*)

Some insectivorous lizards, particularly burrowing or fossorial species, love earthworms and others hate them. The best way to find out whether or not your lizard will go for earthworms is to try them. Some lizards may eat them if the body slime is rinsed off. Earthworms shouldn't be fed too often as their fat content is high.

As tempting as it may be, never use earthworms you find in your own yard. These worms absorb toxins from their surroundings and because you don't know where wild-caught worms have been, it is a risky procedure to feed them to your reptiles. Cultured worms can be purchased in most bait shops and in starter cultures from mail-order sources. They are easy to breed and can be fed a variety of common household foods such as milk-soaked bread, raw white potato and leftover vegetables from last night's dinner. Because of their moist skin, they serve as excellent vehicles for vitamin/mineral powders, which adhere to them quite easily. Some lizards may not like the taste of these additions but will eat the worm in its natural form. In this case you can fool your lizard by gut loading the worm or injecting it with a vitamin/mineral preparation suspended in solution.

Feeding Larger Carnivores

Larger lizards such as monitors, tegus and other carnivores will eat insects but need so many to make a meal that it is more efficient to feed them larger prey such as rodents. As mentioned in chapter 6, some monitors and tegus can be encouraged to eat cooked meats and canned foods.

Few but the very largest monitors are capable of eating rats or full grown chickens. However, many intermediate sized carnivorous lizards eat mice and chicks. Mice are an excellent food because they contain an abundance of protein, vitamins and minerals, and because they eat virtually anything, it is not difficult to gut load them for the benefit of your lizards. Deciding what size food your lizard can handle is accomplished by determining with your eye the size of its gape and feeding it items about half, but no more than three-quarters, of the gape diameter. Of course smaller items are easily taken as well.

This Savannah Monitor is polishing off a tasty mouse meal.

The question often arises whether one should feed live or dead mice to mouse-eating lizards and snakes. Virtually every zoo in the world feeds nothing but pre-killed and usually frozen (and thawed out) rodents to their reptiles. If you throw a live mouse or rat (other than a newborn) into a cage with a lizard or snake you risk injury to the reptile. Live rodents will fight back when attacked. And some lizards disinterested in attacking or fighting with the rodent may find themselves being nibbled on instead. In addition, rodents frozen for several weeks at low temperatures are free of parasites that could infect your reptile had it eaten the rodent alive or freshly killed. All rodent-eating lizards are also carrion eaters, so a thawed out, previously frozen mouse should present no problem for them. It is also possible to inject or otherwise dose the dead mouse with a vitamin/mineral mixture, which the lizard won't notice because it eats the animal whole. So there aren't any good reasons to feed your reptile a live mouse when a frozen one, properly thawed and vitamin supplemented, will do much better.

Feeding Herbivorous Lizards

Herbivorous lizards such as iguanids, mastigures and others have special dietary needs. It is not good enough to throw in a few sprigs of lettuce or spinach and hope for the best. Herbivores need proteins, vitamins, calcium, phosphorous and other minerals normally found in the diet of carnivores. You can ensure that your herbivorous lizard is getting everything it needs nutritionally by feeding the right mix of fruits and vegetables.

THE LOVE OF LETTUCE

Many lizards, such as iguanas, love to eat lettuce. If given lettuce, they may shun other more nutritional foods. Rather than set your lizard up for malnourishment, your best bet is to avoid feeding lettuce. By doing so, you will prevent the development of poor eating habits in your lizard.

Alfalfa pellets are available to meet your herbivore's protein requirements. These are a highly concentrated source of plant protein (up to 18 percent), whereas bean and alfalfa sprouts have much less. Sprouts are good for an occasional treat but should not be fed to provide all your herbivore's protein needs. In addition, they have other drawbacks, including a low calcium to phosphorus ratio. Ideally the ratio of calcium to phosphorus should be two to one. Some people will advise using hard-boiled egg, yogurt, cheese and even milk as a source of protein, but unfortunately herbivorous lizards do not have the digestive enzymes to properly break down dairy products, so these items will cause nothing but grief for your lizard. Good alternative sources of plant protein include navy, kidney, lima, red, black and pinto beans. They should be cooked and mashed and added to the salad you prepare for your plant-eating lizards. Beans are high in phosphorus and low in calcium, but this is easily remedied by adding a calcium supplement to the mash.

Collard greens are a healthy staple for your herbivorous lizard. (Green Iguana)

There are many vegetables that can cause problems when fed in excess. These include plants containing an excess of oxalates such as broccoli, spinach and parsley. Some greens that contain lesser amounts of oxalates are good for other reasons. These include collards, carrots, squash, sweet potato and turnips. Spinach, beets, rhubarb and Swiss chard are high in oxalic acid, and this in turn can lead to hardening of the internal organs, a condition known as visceral gout. Oxalates also bind to calcium, making it unavailable for bone growth and replacement.

The following greens should be fed daily: collard, mustard, dandelion and escarole. Mustard and dandelion greens can also be fed with their flowers, which are a special treat for herbivores. Green Iguanas also relish hibiscus flowers, but offer these as a treat only. These are available to some iguana owners living in places where these flowers are grown. If you feed any flowers or greens collected outdoors, be absolutely certain that there are no pesticides, weed killers or chemical fertilizers in the ground from which they were picked.

With the exception of animals that eat fruits in the wild, apples, bananas, pears and citrus should be fed only in small amounts and as a special treat once a week or less. Fruits are low in calcium but high in phosphorus. Bananas are particularly high in potassium and iguanas will gorge themselves on this fruit, developing an electrolyte imbalance in the process. Excessive potassium can cause heart problems and cardiac arrest.

Iguanas and other herbivores may become fixated on one kind of vegetable; this is why it's important to start off feeding a variety so they don't become accustomed to one type to the exclusion of all others. For example, all forms of lettuce (Romaine, Iceberg, Bib, Green/Red Leaf, etc.) are nutritionally worthless. But given a choice, iguanas will munch on the tender, sweet tasting leaves of lettuce and pass up anything else, including foods that they need to remain healthy.

Over the years there has been considerable debate over whether or not herbivorous lizards such as the Green Iguana should be fed animal protein as they will accept mealworms, insects and even prepared animal

A SAMPLE SALAD

A typical herbivorous lizard salad, which you can make up as you go or process on a grander scale and store in the refrigerator, includes the following items and proportions:

> $\frac{1}{2}$ cup raw green beans, diced or shredded
>
> $\frac{1}{2}$ cup raw yellow or green squash
>
> $\frac{1}{4}$ cup shredded or julienned carrot
>
> $\frac{1}{2}$ to 1 cup alfalfa pellets (all feedings)
>
> Less than $\frac{1}{4}$ cup apple, pear, banana (choose one) as a garnish

Garnish lightly with other fruits: strawberries, raspberries, papaya, mango, plums, apricots and figs, either fresh or dried.

Add a vitamin/mineral supplement sprinkled as a powder and thoroughly mix up in the salad. Spray the mixture lightly with water prior to feeding, as an extra source of fluids for your lizards. Mastigures get most if not all their water from the food they eat; other herbivores may drink from a water bowl but benefit from fluids in or on food as well.

protein food such as monkey biscuits and other animal chows. Proponents of the animal protein diet point to the fact that juvenile animals have allegedly been observed eating animal matter in the wild, although this has never been proven except as an occasional aberrant behavior. Opponents point to the fact that animal-based foods not only cause visceral gout in iguanas, but also cause kidney failure due to high levels of uric acid associated with such diets. A good part of this debate concerns the fact that herbivores in captivity are more apt to develop meta-

Some lizards, like this Malagasy Lines Gecko, will not drink their water out of a bowl, but instead lick condensation from their faces and nearby leaves. For these lizards, regular misting is necessary.

bolic bone disease. Some scientists say it is impossible for them to obtain the calcium and phosphorus they need in proper proportions, or to adequately synthesize vitamin D3 on a plant-based diet alone, even with the requisite UV-B light available. Vitamin D3 is needed to mineralize and remineralize bone. The current consensus, however, is that it is possible to feed herbivores a nutritionally adequate diet and to provide them with either natural or artificial sources of UV-B without fear of developing dreaded MBD, metabolic bone disease. The use of vitamin/mineral supplement powders formulated specially for such lizards is a necessary ingredient in this scheme. The importance of this research goes beyond the keeping of herbivorous lizards successfully and may contribute to our knowledge of human bone development and regrowth.

Feeding Omnivorous Lizards

There are few omnivorous lizards, species that eat a combination of both animal and vegetable matter. Probably one of the most popular to the hobbyist is the Bearded Dragon (*Pogona sp.*). Dragon lizards feed on a variety of invertebrates that they are capable of subduing and ingesting, including most insects. When they get larger (up to 24 inches including tail) they will eat other, smaller lizards. They should be offered vegetable as well as animal matter regularly. Beardeds are fond of almost any animate invertebrate as well as berries, tangerine, bits of collards and green beans that have been diced into bite size pieces.

chapter 9

Keeping Your Lizard Healthy

Having a healthy lizard starts when you select it at the pet store, reptile swap meet or at a breeder's facility. It is not a good idea to buy your lizards by mail unless you buy from a reliable dealer who is willing to guarantee the animal. Start the

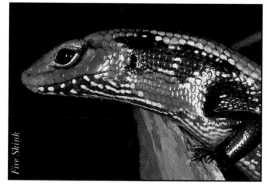

Fire Skink

inspection process by examining the animal carefully. Check to see that it's active, eats readily (ask that it be fed in front of you) and is otherwise behaving normally. Examine the eyes and nasal region for signs of mucus or discharge. Ask to hold the lizard that you've selected. Turn it over and the examine the anal vent. It should be clean and free of any fecal matter or adherences. Examine the skin carefully for the presence of mites or ticks and any patches of flaky or dried, unshed skin, sores or ulcerations. A small pocket magnifier can help you make your examination. After all, jewelers use them

107

when buying gemstones, so why not when buying a living gem of your own? If any of the above conditions are present, it's a good idea to stay away from the animal as much as you might be attracted to it. Any unusual swellings or knots under the skin are another reason to pass up a particular lizard, although you could be holding a gravid female full of eggs.

Having a healthy lizard starts with picking the right specimen. (Giant Day Gecko)

Eating Disorders

The most common health problems of captive lizards are usually related to diet. Nutrition information has been discussed in detail in chapter 8, but regardless of how well you feed your lizard, if it won't eat, it is urgent that you find the cause and correct it as soon as possible. The causes of anorexia in lizards that are habitat-related include:

1. Inadequate temperature control. Temperatures may be either too high or too low.

2. Improper humidity levels. Some species require a dry environment, others need a humid environment.

3. Handling of shy and retiring species may cause such animals to stop feeding.

4. The stress of too small an enclosure or overcrowding. Cage mates can stress each other over territory.

5. Lack of suitable substrate for burrowing or fossorial lizards and lack of a suitable hidebox for animals that wish to escape daylight. This invariably leads to stress and anorexia.

6. Improper correlation of temperature and day/night cycles. Diurnal or daylight animals require higher temperatures during their photoperiod and a drop in temperature during the dark part of the cycle.

7. Offering food that is either not normally accepted by the species or that is prepared or offered in a manner the lizard may find unacceptable for reasons we cannot begin to fathom.

Medical reasons for anorexia include:

1. Pregnancy. Gravid females tend to eat less or not at all until after they expel their eggs.

2. Infectious diseases including viral, bacterial and parasitic diseases. These are discussed below.

3. Metabolic bone disease may cause a condition known as rubber jaw, which softens bones of the head and loosens teeth. This makes eating extremely difficult, if not impossible.

4. Cancer. Lizards can get tumors, and these eventually interfere with the dietary intake.

Overcrowding may result in lack of appetite in your lizards. These young Bearded Dragons will be separated shortly to prevent territorial battles between juveniles.

Regardless of cause, anorexia invariably leads to weight loss, lethargy, immune system depression and death from starvation. Finding the cause and correcting it is crucial. If experimenting with environmental conditions fails to solve the problem, it's necessary to consult a veterinarian experienced with captive reptiles.

Two other symptoms of gastrointestinal problems are vomiting and diarrhea. Because lizards have an extremely well-developed muscular sphincter, vomiting is a rarity among them. If you see your lizard regurgitating, this is a sign that it needs *immediate* veterinary attention. Causes can include overwhelming sepsis or infection, a foreign body in the gastrointestinal tract and gastrointestinal tract obstructions due to intestinal parasite overload or enlarged liver or kidneys.

DIARRHEA

Diarrhea can be a symptom of something as simple as inadequate temperature levels, which in turn result in incomplete digestion of food matter. Diarrhea can also be dietary; feeding excessive amounts of foods with high water content, dog food, raw chicken, eggs and other meat products may also result in diarrhea. Diarrhea can also be caused by bacterial agents and parasites. Salmonella is endemic to many animals, including 90 percent of all reptiles. It is rarely a problem, but stress and immune system depression due to a variety of factors can lead to an overgrowth of this organism, which then results in diarrhea symptoms. Salmonella is discussed in more detail below. Parasites that can cause dysentery in lizards include hookworms, roundworms, amoebas and other one-celled or multicellular organisms. These need to be professionally diagnosed and treated.

Viral diseases are rare in lizards; however, lizards may contract paromyxoviruses and inclusion body disease due to viral pathogens, first seen in snakes, may be contagious to lizards. While there is no cure for such diseases, they can be prevented by quarantining new animals from existing specimens in your collection for several weeks and by not keeping suspect snakes in close proximity to lizards. Bacterial and parasite diseases are infinitely more common in these reptiles and fortunately both these maladies are often readily amenable to veterinary treatment.

Externally visible bacterial infections often take the form of abscesses as well as a condition known as dry gangrene, which can occur where tail joints have separated due to an autotomy episode. The remaining end of the tail begins to die and turns dark brown or black and then hardens. Dry gangrene and abscesses need to be attended to by a veterinarian who can surgically remove contaminated tissue and treat the animal with antibiotics.

Reptile Associated Salmonellosis

Salmonella in reptiles has been known since at least 1947. Since then there have been numerous studies that have concluded that more than 90 percent of all reptiles are symptomless carriers of various types of this bacteria. Salmonella is ubiquitous in our environment. It is not only present in a wide variety of foods we humans eat but is carried by insects, fish, amphibians and other vertebrates as well as reptiles. From the mid 1960s to early 1970s, more than a quarter of a million young children and babies became ill with salmonella, which was traced to baby turtles that they were given as pets. As a result, the U.S. government banned the sale of turtles with shell lengths of less than 4 inches, except for scientific research or legitimate educational use. More recently, lizards, notably the common Green Iguana, gained unfavorable media publicity as the transmittor of salmonella in numerous cases throughout the U.S. and overseas. At least two newborn infants perished as a result of complications from the disease, which they obtained from their mothers who, in turn, obtained it from pet iguanas in their households. Iguana pets kept in day-care centers and homes with young children were being implicated in infections among their young handlers. There are facts that all would-be and current lizard fanciers should be aware of with respect to the threat of reptile-associated salmonella.

> **BE AWARE OF SALMONELLA**
>
> All victims of a recent salmonella outbreak in Denver, Colorado had a few things in common which pointed to reptiles as the source of the infection. They all visited the Denver Zoo, all had eaten finger food there (hot dogs, hamburgers or sandwiches) and all had touched or pressed up against the railing of the Komodo Dragon Lizard (*Varanus komodiensis*) exhibit. The same serotype of salmonella that these victims had was cultured off the railing. This proved that even surfaces, without the reptile present, could be responsible for salmonella infection.

1. All reptiles should be considered infected with salmonella.

2. Because it isn't always shed in the feces, a negative culture does not mean the animal is free of the bacteria.

3. Unless it is causing diarrhea and other symptoms in reptiles, it should *never* be treated by antibiotics just because it is present.

4. It must never be treated, without veterinary supervision, using antibiotics one can obtain in pet shops designed for tropical fish.

5. Treating symptomless salmonella in reptiles is harmful to the reptile and potentially dangerous to humans. In order to wipe out the salmonella, the gut is also made free of other bacteria the animal needs to help digest food matter. In addition, treatment leads to the emergence of resistant forms of salmonella, which could make later treatment of infected humans more difficult if not impossible.

PEOPLE AT RISK FROM SALMONELLA

1. Most healthy people and older children who become infected with salmonella rarely suffer more than one or two days of stomach discomfort, diarrhea and, on occasion, nausea and vomiting. The infection is self-limiting and doctors treat it only if it persists for more than two days. You can prevent illness with reptile-associated salmonella by scrubbing the hands thoroughly for a minimum of thirty seconds with an antibacterial soap and hot water.

2. Infants (including unborn babies), toddlers and children up to the age of eight may suffer more serious problems with salmonella infection. The vast majority of salmonella associated fatalities occur in infants and small children. Therefore, under no circumstances should babies and young children be allowed contact with reptiles. Older children must be rigidly instructed to wash thoroughly after handling a reptile and before touching their faces or eating food of any kind.

3. Adults and older children handling reptiles must never touch a baby or younger child before washing hands thoroughly. Direct contact between the reptile and an infant is not necessary for the infant to become infected. Infection can be transmitted to the infant by an intermediary such as a parent or older sibling.

4. Anyone who is handling food must never do so after having contact with any reptile, its caging or supplies, without first washing hands thoroughly.

5. Be especially cognizant of the possibility of infection when away from home—at the zoo or a swap meet, for example. Many people at reptile swap meets think nothing of examining and handling a potential purchase and then swinging by the snack bar for a hamburger or hot dog, immeasurably increasing the potential for contracting salmonella. Visit the rest room or use any one of a number of disinfectant hand washes now available for use away from the convenience of a bathroom sink.

Children can enjoy a lizard pet, like this Blue-tongued Skink, immensely. Make sure children are supervised while handling the animals and thoroughly disinfect their hands afterwards.

6. Besides infants and young children, other categories are also at risk from more serious consequences of salmonella infection. Anyone who is immunocompromised for any reason— be it AIDS, chemotherapy, radiation treatment or steroid and other medical treatment—is especially susceptible. The elderly and frail may also have decreased immunity to the effects of salmonella. Such individuals, if they have contact with a reptile or anything the reptile touched, must be especially obsessive about washing and disinfecting the hands thoroughly afterwards.

Salmonella does not have to be a problem if simple, commonsense hygienic measures are taken. Besides hand washing, the following measures should be adopted for any reptile related operation:

1. If possible, always use a basement slop sink for reptile-related cleaning operations. If a bathroom sink must be used, remove all articles of personal hygiene such as toothpaste, tooth- and hair brushes, razors, etc. Afterwards, thoroughly disinfect the sink and countertops before returning these articles. The same procedures apply to a kitchen sink used for reptile cleaning chores. Remove all cutlery, dishes, dish racks, sponges used for dish washing and so on. Then disinfect the sink and countertops before putting these items back.

2. Always keep your reptile's enclosure as clean and free from waste matter as possible. If necessary, don disposable rubber gloves and remove all fecal matter daily or every other day. Change the water in the water bowl daily or every other day as well. Be sure to wash your hands after these chores.

After you handle your lizard, scrub your hands with antibacterial soap and hot water. (Giant Gecko)

A Word About Hand Washing

Rinsing alone in cool water will not eliminate salmonella germs. It is necessary to scrub the hands thoroughly with disinfectant soap and hot water. Studies done in hospitals also indicate that you should wash the hands for at least thirty seconds to ensure complete disinfection.

Choosing a Reptile Veterinarian

Many veterinarians are dog and cat experts, but doctors experienced with reptiles are rather few and far between. However, more and more vets are becoming members of the Association of Amphibian and Reptile Veterinarians and are learning more about reptiles every day. The first thing to do is to call around to find a vet not too far away who may have experience with reptiles—if you don't find one, then try to find a vet who is at least willing to care for your reptiles and who could consult over the phone with more qualified experts on reptile health problems.

Many lizards, including iguanas, can live twenty years or longer if properly fed, housed and otherwise cared for. Professional veterinary care is a necessary part of that equation and must not be overlooked.

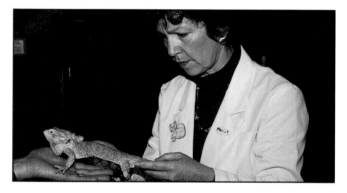

Try to find a veterinarian who has some experience treating reptiles. (Bearded Dragon)

WHAT HAPPENS AT THE VET

It is likely that the first thing your vet will do is a flotation test. In this test, a sample of the animals feces is suspended in solution. If any parasites are present, their eggs, will float to the surface. The surface fluid is skimmed off the tube and examined under a microscope. Every kind of parasite has distinctive looking eggs, and a diagnosis can be made by your vet, who will then prescribe the right medicine and the right dosages to eliminate them.

Your vet will also perform a physical exam, which involves listening to your lizard's heart and lungs, palpating or feeling for unusual lumps and performing a visual inspection of the skin, anal region, eyes, nostrils and mouth. The doctor can also feel the bones to determine if metabolic bone disease is present or in an early stage of development.

115

Reproduction Related Problems

By far the most common reproductive problem female lizards endure is egg binding or dystocia. It also occurs in snakes, turtles and crocodilians. It is most common in first-time breeding females, females with a history of the problem in previous seasons and females with a history of producing non-fertile eggs.

Egg binding is the inability of the eggs to pass through the ovicust and cloaca. Passage may be impaired by obstructions such as infectious abscesses or cysts, two or even three eggs that have become fused together into one large unpassable mass or one or more unusually large or over-developed eggs. Even in the absence of physical obstruction, dystocia may occur due to a variety of factors including poor nutrition, suboptimal temperatures (which limit metabolic activity in general), dehydration, obesity, poor physical condition and other diseases such as parasite or bacterial infections that compromise the animal's overall health. Environmental causes of dystocia, in addition to suboptimal temperatures, may also include the absence of a suitable nesting site or substrate. Captive lizards that lay their eggs in soil just beneath the surface in the wild may not be provided with an equivalent option and will begin digging motions that are to no avail. Recognizing this symptom and correcting the problem by moving the animal to an aquarium lined with sterile potting soil can sometimes be the simplest solution to the problem, in addition to providing adequate humidity and temperature levels.

If nothing you can do alleviates the problem, a visit to a veterinarian is in order. The condition can be fatal if not resolved, but there are several treatments available. The veterinarian can inject the lizard with a drug

HOW TO FIND A VETERINARIAN

Although many veterinarians are reluctant to treat lizards, it is important that you know who to call in case of an emergency. Don't wait until your lizard needs medical attention to find a vet schooled in reptiles. A great place to inquire is your local herpetological society. This group will be able to point you in the direction of veterinarians with the requisite background and interest in your pet.

called pitocin, which will induce muscular contractions that can force the eggs out. There are several varieties of this drug that may be used in conjunction with other hormones. The veterinarian can also aspirate the contents of the eggs (sacrificing them as a result) and they are passed essentially as waste matter. If they are not passed within two days after this procedure, the next option is the lizard equivalent of a cesarean section.

Physical Injuries

Lizards can become physically injured in a number of ways. They can lose claws by catching them on something, become burned by getting too close to a heat source or become traumatically injured in a fight with a cagemate or in an attempt to escape. A common injury is rubbed-nose in lizards that try to nose their way out of an enclosure by rubbing them on screening or in a corner. These injuries can usually be treated without veterinary intervention by using beta-dine and antibiotic ointments purchased over the counter in any drugstore. Noserub can progress to more serious bacterial infections such as mouth rot, so it should be attended to promptly. If mouth rot occurs, stronger systemic antibiotics and treatment with special antiseptics, administered by a veterinar-

Good nutrition, necessary veterinary care and a caring owner are essential for a healthy lizard. (Berber Skink)

ian, may be necessary. Serious traumatic injury with bleeding or broken bones also requires follow-up veterinary care.

It can be difficult to know when your lizard needs veterinary attention. This chapter has attempted to present some brief guidelines to help in making that decision. If in doubt, a call or brief visit to your reptile vet is always the safest route to take.

part four

Beyond the Basics

chapter 10

Lizard
Conservation

Out of the several thousand species and sub-species of lizards worldwide, perhaps several hundred are considered seriously endangered. Many more are threatened or are of special concern to conservationists because of dwindling numbers and habitat destruction. While collecting lizards from the  wild for the pet trade puts pressure on remaining animals to survive, many lizard species are threatened by other reasons including the following:

HABITAT DESTRUCTION

Natural disaster and human activities like clear cutting of forests, pollution of water supplies, agricultural projects and human (residential) encroachment result in habitat destruction.

DISEASE

Most reptiles in the wild live in harmony with their parasites, including otherwise pathogenic bacteria, viruses and protozoans. However, unknown stresses can impair immune status and cause population declines for no apparent reason. While never clearly documented for lizards, unknown disease factors have been reliably suspected as the reason for extinctions and population declines in other reptiles and amphibians.

OVER-COLLECTING

Lizards are much in demand. In some societies they are eaten and are an important source of protein for native peoples. Their hides are used to make wallets, shoes, belts and other luxury goods, so collecting specimens for this purpose provides much needed money and income for low-income indigenous peoples. Many species are also in demand for the pet trade, particularly the lizards that are preferred because of temperament, coloration, size or other unusual features or markings. Collecting for the pet trade can also result in population decimation. Some of the more popular and expensive types of rare lizards are regularly smuggled and then re-sold as captive-born. These are frequently "laundered" through a second or even a third country before they reach the pet markets in countries like the U.S.

WHAT IS CITES?

CITES stands for the Convention on the International Trade in Endangered Species. It is an international agreement known also as the Washington Treaty, signed by over 120 nations and ratified by the U.S. in 1975.

CITES protects endangered species, both those in immediate danger of extinction (CITES Appendix I) and those whose numbers are declining (CITES Appendix II). It is illegal for anyone to import or export CITES Appendix I species, except zoos with special permits. It is illegal for anyone to import or export CITES Appendix II species unless they were captured by special permit or were bred in captivity.

What Is Being Done About Lizard Conservation?

In the United States, a few species of lizards have state or Federal Endangered Species status, which means they can't be collected, possessed or traded in any way whatsoever. Gila Monsters are one of these protected species. Others include less popular species such as skinks, collared lizards and legless species. Most wildlife protection laws have provisions that permit breeders of captive-held endangered species to possess and trade in these species under a permitting system. Private breeders who produce lizards for the pet trade help to remove at least one threat on wild populations—the over-collecting of a species for that trade. On an international level, the trade in lizards and other threatened or endangered species is governed by an international treaty known as CITES (Convention International Trade in Endangered Species).

Can Captive Breeding Help?

This is a debatable subject. Lizards bred in captivity are rarely if ever rereleased in the wild to repopulate habitats where they once existed. There are a number of important reasons for this. All too often the habitat is gone or spoiled, so that reintroduction would be of no help anyway. In addition, captive-bred and -raised lizards may not be immune to infectious diseases encountered in the wild and might soon die. In addition, captive-bred and -raised lizards may carry bacteria to which they have immunities, but to which their wild cousins do not. This could seriously imperil whatever wild remaining lizards there may be. Because of these reasons, under no circumstances should captive lizards ever be considered for release into the wild. And releasing a species that is not native can also cause a serious upset in the balance of nature. Released non-native animals may be more effective competitors for

In the United States, a few species, such as the Eastern Collared Lizard, enjoy the protection of the Endangered Species Act.

the same food sources as the native species, crowding them out or even preying on them. Florida has been a popular state for these alien species due to its hospitable climate; there are all manner of non-native species there which, in many cases, have outgunned native species for food and territory. Lizards are well represented among these interlopers.

Although captive-bred specimens are rarely released back into the wild, they can take pressure off wild stocks. (Common Chameleon)

One thing is certain, however: Captive-bred lizards of certain popular and fecund species that have become enormously popular as pets (e.g. Australian Bearded Dragons and Green Iguanas), or as pets and as a source of food (Green Iguanas), have taken away the enormous pressure commerce would place on them in the wild were they not so easy to breed or even commercially "farm" (as in the case of iguanas). This is not necessarily true for lizards that are more difficult to breed in captivity. These lizards command such high prices that wild-caught animals remain far less expensive. This competitive edge, unfortunately, keeps the demand for the wild caught of such species above projected sustainable levels, and this is when legal protective measures often must come into play.

chapter 11

Resources

Publications

The Herpetology Source Book and Directory

This is a 400 page listing of every conceivable service or product provider a reptile or amphibian hobbyist would ever need. It includes state laws, lists reptile-experienced veterinarians by state and names live animal and food dealers and a host of other services and suppliers. This company also publishes the Reptile and Amphibian Magazine *eight times yearly. It is available from:*

Reptile and Amphibian Magazine
Box 3709-A, RD 3, Rte. 61 Hwy.
Pottsville, PA 17901
(717) 622-6050

Vivarium Magazine
This is the official magazine of the American Federation of Herpetoculturists and contains a wealth of information on the hobby of herpetoculture. Edited by a veterinarian specializing in amphibians and reptiles. Vivarium *is available from:*

American Federation Of Herpetoculturists
P.O. Box 300067
Escondido, CA 92030-0067
(619) 747-4948

Veterinary Services for Reptiles

A member of the Association of Reptilian and Amphibian Veterinarians can be located by contacting the association at the address below. Membership is also open to nonvets interested in herpetology, and includes a bulletin and directory. In addition to the U.S., there are chapters in Europe and Australia.

For information contact:

Wilber B. Amand, VMD
Box 605
Chester Heights, PA 19017
(610) 892-4812

Internet Resources

Links to a wide variety of on-line resources dealing with reptiles and amphibians, including health-related concerns, care and keeping and conservation issues, can be obtained on the World Wide Web by bookmarking and using the following Web site doorway address:

http://www.xmission.com/~gastown/herpmed/

Note: There is a special lizard subsection that readers can jump to in order to narrow their search of the Web to lizard relevant information.

Live Food/Nutritional Supplements

Rep-Cal
(800) 406-6446
(408) 356-4289

Manufacturers of nutritional vitamin and mineral supplements for reptiles. Owned and operated under the management of a physician.

Bassetts Cricket Ranch, Inc.
(800) 634-2445

Zoophobias, mealworms, crickets (all sizes).

Top Hat Cricket Farm, Inc.
(800) 638-2555

Crickets (all sizes), mealworms, superworms, waxworms, cricket food and cricket caging/handling materials.

Ghann's Cricket Farm, Inc.
(800) 476-2248

Crickets (all sizes), mealworms, superworms, cricket feed, supplies and accessories.

Armstrong's Cricket Farm
(800) 658-3409

Crickets (all sizes), superworms, giant mealworms, mealworms, waxworms. All accessories.

Nature's Way
(800) 318-2611

Mealworms, giant mealworms, waxworms, fly larva and all sizes of crickets.

Drosophila
(800) 545-2303

Flightless, USDA approved interstate shipment of fruit fly cultures (several species). All supplies and culture media and instructional material for culturing fruit flies.

SAS Rodents
(518) 537-2000

Fresh frozen rodents from pinkie sized mice to jumbo rats.

Lam Distributing
(903) 683-512

Fresh frozen mice and rats. All sizes.

The Mouse House
(717) 622-7850

Wholesale/retail quantities of fresh frozen feeder mice. All sizes. Operated under veterinary supervision.

Rainbow Mealworms
(800) 777-9676

Mealworms and crickets. All sizes. Wholesale and bulk packed.

Grubo
(800) 222-3563

Mealworms, fly larva, waxworms, superworms and crickets. All sizes.

Arbico
(800) 827-2847

Provides a wide variety of live insects for feeding purposes and agricultural use.